Reading and Interpreting the Works of

EDGAR ALLAN POE

Enslow Publishing
101 W. 23rd Street
Suite 240
New York, NY 10011
USA
enslow.com

Lit Crit
Guides

Reading and Interpreting
the Works of

EDGAR
ALLAN POE

Debra McArthur

Published in 2016 by Enslow Publishing, LLC
101 W. 23rd Street, Suite 240, New York, NY 10011

Library of Congress Cataloging-in-Publication Data

McArthur, Debra.
 Reading and interpreting the works of Edgar Allan Poe / Debra McArthur.
  pages cm. — (Lit crit guides)
 Includes bibliographical references and index.
 Summary: "Describes the life and work of writer Edgar Allan Poe"— Provided by publisher.
 ISBN 978-0-7660-7342-5
 1. Poe, Edgar Allan, 1809-1849—Juvenile literature. 2. Poe, Edgar Allan, 1809-1849—Criticism and interpretation. 3. Authors, American—19th century—Biography—Juvenile literature. I. Title.
 PS2631.M378 2016
 818'.309—dc23
 [B]
                            2015028591

Printed in the United States of America

To Our Readers: We have done our best to make sure all website addresses in this book were active and appropriate when we went to press. However, the author and the publisher have no control over and assume no liability for the material available on those websites or on any websites they may link to. Any comments or suggestions can be sent by e-mail to customerservice@enslow.com.

Portions of this book originally appeared in *A Student's Guide to Edgar Allan Poe.*

CONTENTS

Edgar Allan Poe

POE: GENIUS OR "JINGLE MAN"?

Few Americans would fail to recognize these lines:

*Once upon a midnight dreary, while I pondered, weak
and weary,
Over many a quaint and curious volume of forgotten lore*[1]

"The Raven" by Edgar Allan Poe is one of the most well-known poems in all of American literature. It is not only a favorite for read-aloud programs at Halloween, but has also been used as the basis for dozens of films, television shows, stories, comics, musical compositions, and even advertisements. But this poem is just one small part of a legacy that continues to fascinate audiences today. Poe is so much a part of popular culture that his "virtual voice" even appears in several Twitter feeds. In many ways Poe's own life was as mysterious as the stories he wrote. He was often the subject of gossip and rumors during his life; after his death even more so. In fact, the very circumstances of his death are still a mystery, one that may never be solved.

Poe and Romanticism

Poe's literary style places him among the Romantics of American literature. This does not mean that he wrote only about romantic love. Romantic literature was a popular form of writing in the early to middle 1800s. It placed more importance on emotion than reason, and dealt with psychology and the inner struggles of the individual. Nature was important to the Romantic writer, especially in the way it affected the spiritual side of man. Many Romantic writers were also interested in the mysterious or even the occult, and had a preoccupation with the spirit of man and perhaps its immortality.

These ideas all play an important role in the works of Poe, but Poe's Romanticism is somewhat different from other authors of his day. According to Dr. Lei Jin, Poe falls into the category of "Dark Romanticism," which she describes as pessimistic, in contrast with the optimistic view of most Romantics. "In Poe's poetry," she says, "the ideal beauty and harmony of nature is either beyond reach or manifests and disappears suddenly like a shooting star, and the poet is left forever tormented by the agony."[2]

Romanticism

A style of literature from the early nineteenth century that features the quest for beauty, imaginative plots which may include the supernatural, and emotion over reason.

Poe's career as a published writer lasted about twenty years, ending with his death in 1849. Although this was before the Civil War, it was a time when the differences in attitudes between North and South were growing. While this conflict of ideas was most obvious in the politics of the time, it also affected the literature of the country.

Poe spent much of his life in Richmond, Virginia, and considered himself a Southerner. During these pre-Civil War times, the South was steeped in its conservative traditions of aristocracy, religion, and even slavery. It was a society that respected the past and also the literature and culture of Europe.

Poe and the Transcendentalists

The literary center of the United States, however, was in New England. The new philosophy sweeping New England at this time was Transcendentalism. Transcendentalists rejected many traditional religious beliefs and were sometimes thought of as "mystics." They were also strong opponents of slavery. In some ways, Transcendentalist literature was similar to Romanticism.

Transcendentalist writers emphasized nature in their writings, but they placed an almost religious significance on it, often describing nature as a way for a person to connect with God. Among the Transcendentalists were Ralph Waldo Emerson, Henry David Thoreau, Walt Whitman, and John Greenleaf Whittier.

Poe's work stands in contrast to the writings of the Transcendentalists. Many Southern writers like Poe dismissed the ideas of Transcendentalism because of its rejection of important traditions of religion and literature. Poe jokingly referred to Transcendentalists as "frogpondians" in some of his letters. Transcendentalists sometimes regarded Romantics like Poe as being too conventional. Emerson once called Poe "the jingle man."

Transcendentalism

A philosophy and style of literature that became popular in the mid-nineteenth century. Transcendentalists believed that the individual should search for truth through meditation that goes beyond reason to put him in touch with nature and with a universal spirituality.

Despite these attitudes, good writers from each group respected the talents of the other. Although Poe did not care for Transcendentalism, he did praise some work of Emerson and other Transcendentalists. Whitman both praised and crit-

American poet Ralph Waldo Emerson was a member of the Transcendentalists, writers and philosophers whose rejection of traditional religion often placed them at odds with Romantics like Poe.

icized Poe when he wrote, "Poe's verses illustrate an intense faculty for technical and abstract beauty, with the rhyming art to excess, an incorrigible propensity toward nocturnal themes . . . and probably belong among the electric lights of imaginative literature, brilliant and dazzling, but with no heat."[3]

Despite the criticism Poe received at the hands of the Transcendentalists, there is no denying that he was a man of extraordinary versatility. His work ranged from lyric poetry to literary criticism. He thrilled readers with the horror of gruesome murders and the rationality of a brilliant detective. His writings have survived the test of time and remain popular with readers of today.

> **lyric poetry**
>
> A short poem that expresses intense feeling. May be set to music.

Melancholy and Madness

Poe's subjects and settings are characteristic of Romantic literature. Many of Poe's stories are similar to the Gothic Romances of English literature, and are set in castles, dungeons, catacombs, and old mansions. The spooky atmosphere of the setting is often magnified by violent storms.

Many of Poe's stories are tales of death. Sometimes it is a murder committed in an act of revenge, as in "The Cask of Amontillado," or an act of madness or hatred, as in "The Tell-Tale Heart." Along with this preoccupation with death, Poe also explored the theme of return from the grave. This may be what a narrator most wishes for, but also finds most frightening, as in "The Raven," "Ligeia," and other stories. Similarly, Poe's stories sometimes include the burial of people who are not really dead, as in "The Fall of the House of Usher," "The Premature Burial," and "The Cask of Amontillado."

Poe's stories, whether in poetry or prose, often involve the death of a beautiful woman who is mourned by someone who loves her. In his essay "The Philosophy of Composition," Poe told about his process of composing "The Raven," but his comments also apply to many of his short stories as well. "Melancholy is thus the most legitimate of all the poetic tones," he stated.[4] Poe went on to explain that "Death, then, of a beautiful woman is, unquestionably, the most poetical topic in the world—and equally is it beyond doubt that the lips best suited for such topic are those of a bereaved lover."[5]

Another element in many of Poe's stories is madness. Poe frequently forces the reader to question the perceptions of his main characters. As he does in 'The Raven,' he often uses narrators whose voices are calm and reasonable at first, but later become more agitated and less reliable. In this way, Poe creates a blurry line between sanity and madness, so that the reader must wonder whether the beating hearts and visions of dead lovers are real or imagined.

Poe often uses symbolism to create a deeper level of meaning in his stories and poems. His early poem, 'To Helen,' incorporated names of characters from mythology such as Helen and Psyche to help readers see his meaning. Later, he used the Arabic symbol of death, the raven, to contribute to his narrator's idea that the bird is a bad omen. Other stories employ ticking clocks and beating hearts to show the passage of time that leads all people to death.

Poe as Poet

Poe began writing poetry during his teenage years and continued writing it until the year of his death. His poetic tastes and techniques changed and developed through his career. Some of his earlier works, such as "Tamerlane" and

"Al Aaraaf," are long, rambling, and loosely structured, when compared to the later poems like "The Bells" or "Annabel Lee." The early poems also reflect the types of epic poetry Poe would have studied in his literature classes in school, while the later poems reflect the conflicts of life and storytelling powers of the more mature writer.

As his career progressed, Poe gave public readings of his work. His poetry became much more musical and suited to reading aloud. He used repeating patterns of rhyme and rhythm to engage his audiences. These techniques helped Poe to give very dramatic readings of his works, and he appeared to enjoy these oppor-

symbolism

The use of an object or idea or stand for something else.

epic

A long poem that tells the story of a hero.

tunities for drama. When his fiancée Elmira Royster Shelton attended one of his readings, she commented, "When Edgar read 'The Raven' he became so wildly excited that he frightened me."[6] Poe himself soon became identified with the melancholy, nearly mad genius who narrated so many of his writings.

Poe's Short Stories

Poe refined the short story and influenced its development as a form of literature. Among his "rules" for good fiction: A story should be short enough to read all in one sitting, should end quickly after the climax of the story, and should be unified in creating a single mood, or emotional effect for the reader. Poe especially praised the work of Hawthorne, and used his review of Hawthorne's book *Twice Told Tales* to present the first real definition and guidelines for the short story in 1842. As he explained:

> A skillful literary artist has constructed a tale. If wise, he has not fashioned his thoughts to accommodate his incidents; but having conceived, with deliberate care, a certain unique or single *effect* to be wrought out, he then invents such incidents—he then combines such events as may best aid him in establishing this preconceived effect. . . . In the whole composition there should be no word written, of which the tendency, direct or indirect, is not to the one pre-established design. And by such means, with such care and skill, a picture is at length painted which leaves in the mind of him who contemplates it with a kindred art, a sense of the fullest satisfaction. The idea of the tale has been presented unblemished, because undisturbed; and this is an end unattainable by the novel.[7]

According to biographer and critic Arthur Hobson Quinn, this statement "represents [Poe] at his best critical form. This is really constructive criticism, for all later writers on the art of fiction have had to quote it, and it has become the standard definition of a short story."[8] In his own work, Poe used the techniques he recommended to others. In many of his writings, the effect is one of gloom and dread, and Poe's settings of castles or dilapidated old houses at midnight helped create this mood. Often, as in "The Raven" and "The Fall of the House of Usher," Poe uses disturbances in nature such as violent storms to reflect the emotional disturbances of narrators who are on the brink of madness. He describes these settings so vividly that readers may feel as if they are actually there in the story with the characters. Perhaps that is one reason why so many of Poe's stories have been adapted for film.

Nathaniel Hawthorne, like Poe, was considered one of the Dark Romantics.

Poe's Tales of "Ratiocination"

Poe is often referred to as "father of the modern detective story." Poe's 1841 story "Murders in the Rue Morgue," was a new form of mystery that would become the standard for future writers. Poe introduced several elements that would be used in later mystery fiction: The main character (only later was the term "detective" coined) is not a member of the police force; the crime has either been unsolvable, or has been incorrectly solved; the detective is accompanied by a second character who, like the reader, is amazed at the detective's abilities; the mystery is solved through logic and keen observation (which Poe called "ratiocination"), and the detective explains how he solved the mystery at the end. These same devices would be used several decades later by Sir Arthur Conan Doyle in writing his stories of Sherlock Holmes. They are still commonly used today in the detective stories of movies and television.

Poe's Literary Criticism

Even before he became well-known for his poetry and stories, Poe made a name for himself as a literary critic. He worked for several different literary magazines during his career, beginning with the *Southern Literary Messenger* in Richmond, Virginia. Poe analyzed the works of the popular writers of the day and published reviews of the latest fiction and poetry. Although he often angered writers and the readers who admired them, his reviews were widely read and contributed to the popularity of several of the journals for which he wrote.

Poe's place as a literary critic has been the subject of controversy for many years. Poe sometimes allowed his personal feelings for other writers to influence his evaluation of their work. He often had harsh words for some of the most respected authors of his day, especially those of the New England literary society whom he believed had snubbed him. Author Henry James said that "Poe's judgments are pretentious, spiteful, vulgar," but he also admitted that Poe had "the advantage of being a man of genius, and his intelligence was frequently great."[9] On other occasions, Poe was guilty of unwarranted praise to mediocre poets whom he did not wish to insult. Despite his sometimes poor judgment, Poe's critical insights helped him to develop theories of good poetry and fiction that are still respected today. Twentieth-century critic Edmund Wilson commented, "His literary articles and lectures, in fact, surely constitute the most remarkable body of criticism ever produced in the United States."[10]

Poe's Place in the Literary World

Poe's writing was popular with the public, but not all critics agreed. When Margaret Fuller of the *New York Daily Tribune* reviewed *The Raven and Other Poems*, she had little praise for most of the poems in the book. She commented, "The productions in this volume indicate a power to do something far better." She did, however, call "The Raven" an exception, and said that it showed, "the writer's artistic skill, and is in its way a rare and finished specimen."[11]

Despite his lack of critical popularity in America, Poe had many admirers in Europe. He cultivated a friendship with English poet Elizabeth Barrett, and even dedicated "The Raven" to her. She said, " 'The Raven' has produced a sensation . . . here in England. . . . Some of my friends are taken by the fear of it and some by the music. I hear of persons absolutely haunted by 'the Nevermore.' "[12]

Perhaps Poe's greatest accomplishment was not just in poetry, fiction, or criticism, but in his remarkable combination of all of these. As Vincent Buranelli says:

> A man can enter many fields without justifiably claiming the ownership of any. This is not true of Poe. He has a strong claim to the titles of our best poet, our best short story writer, and our best critic. Whether each of these titles be genuine or not, the overall achievement they represent is not easily challenged by any other American author.[13]

Poe remains one of the most popular writers in American literary history. Readers today are still chilled by the dark dungeons and gloomy castles, the madness of the narrators, and above all, the mysterious, tragic, and often self-destructive character of the man whose imagination created the stately bird of yore with his melancholy refrain of "Nevermore."

THE YOUNG POET

In 1806 actors David and Elizabeth Poe were married in Richmond, Virginia. The couple traveled from place to place, taking stage roles in Baltimore, Philadelphia, and other cities. Their first son, William Henry Leonard Poe, was born in 1807. Times were hard for the family, and the actors found it hard to make enough money to support their family. They were living in Boston, Massachusetts, on January 19, 1809, When Elizabeth gave birth to her second son, Edgar.

Elizabeth, or Eliza as she was known, was well-liked by Boston audiences, and received the praise of theater critics for her singing, dancing, and acting skills.[1] David and Eliza left Boston with their two children during the fall of 1809 to pursue opportunities on the stages of New York. At the end of the season, in July 1810, Eliza Poe left New York to join an acting troupe in Richmond, Virginia, where she had friends. No mention is made of David Poe in any newspaper, theater program, or other historical document after this point. Perhaps he was seriously ill; maybe he simply abandoned the family. According to biographer Hervey Allen, a rumor surfaced that David Poe had left his wife for a Scottish mistress, with whom he later had a son. Allen dismisses this story as false. A newspaper clipping of unknown origin reported David Poe's death on October 19, 1810, but there is no reliable information to verify this.[2]

Poe's mother, Elizabeth, was an actress who died when he was only two years old.

In any case, Eliza now had two small children to support on her own small weekly wages, and was also pregnant with her third child. She gave birth to a daughter she named Rosalie in December 1810. In the summer of 1811, Eliza was seriously ill. By mid-October, she was unable to perform any longer, and so her only source of income was gone. Eliza Poe died December 8, 1811, possibly of either pneumonia or tuberculosis.[3]

Edgar's New Family

During her final days, Eliza and her children were helped by two young Richmond housewives: Mrs. John Allan and Mrs. William McKenzie. When Eliza died, her eldest child, William Henry Poe, was sent to live with his paternal grandparents in Baltimore, and the two Richmond women offered homes to the two younger children. Mrs. McKenzie took the baby, Rosalie, and Mrs. Allan took the toddler Edgar. Even though Edgar received the name "Allan" as his new middle name, he was never legally adopted by the Allans.

John Allan operated a store in Richmond. When international trade opportunities arose, Allan took the family to England. Edgar attended English boarding schools for the next five years, and received an education in Latin and French, as well as dancing, geography, religion, and history.[4] In the summer of 1820, the family returned to Richmond. For the next several years, Edgar attended private schools in Richmond and was a very good student, excelling in Latin and public speaking. He was also very athletic and enjoyed boxing, swimming, and running.[5] Some have suggested that he had a sad and lonely childhood, but according to biographer George Woodberry, "His lot as a boy was a favored one; he was happy, hardy, and healthful, and in his foster-mother,

21

her sister . . . the Mackenzies, and others, he found warm and ready affections."[6]

During Edgar's teenage years, his relationship with John Allan was strained. Allan's business struggled financially, and Allan perhaps resented the expenses of Edgar's schooling and other needs. Biographer Arthur Hobson Quinn suggests that Edgar may also have been aware that his foster father was having an extra-marital affair.[7] Edgar and Allan quarreled often, and in a letter to Edgar's brother Henry, Allan described Edgar as being, "sulky & ill-tempered."[8] In 1825 John Allan's uncle, William Galt, died and left the family money and land. Allan purchased a large house in Richmond, and arranged for Edgar to change schools in order to begin a more intensive course of study to prepare him to attend the newly-opened University of Virginia.

A Short College Career

In February 1826, Edgar left Richmond to attend the University of Virginia in Charlottesville. It was a prestigious institution, and most of Poe's classmates came from wealthy families. Poe studied in two schools at the University: ancient languages and modern languages. He was listed among the top students by both of his professors at the end of the term in December 1826. Unfortunately, that term was his last. Allan claimed that he withdrew Poe from the school because of the young man's drinking and gambling. However, letters from Poe and from the school indicate that Allan had not paid Poe's full expenses at the time he enrolled. Poe was often reminded of the debt by school officials and the hotel-keeper in charge of his dormitory. Poe claimed that he began gambling as a way to increase the small amount of money Allan had given him, in order to cover the expenses of his books and other fees.[9]

Allan refused to allow him to return to the school for another term.

Upon arriving home, Poe was met with another disappointment. His romance with his childhood sweetheart, Elmira Royster, had been ended by her engagement to a Richmond businessman. He would later discover that her father had intercepted the letters Poe sent her from Charlottesville, because he did not consider Poe a worthy match for his daughter. Poe worked briefly in the bookkeeping department of Allan's business before leaving for Boston in April of 1827.

Poe the Soldier

On May 26, Poe enlisted in the Army under the name Edgar A. Perry. He gave his age as twenty-two, although he was only eighteen. Private Perry was assigned to the First Artillery unit at Fort Independence, in Boston Harbor. Shortly after his enlistment, Poe had a small book of poems entitled *Tamerlane*

POE AT UVA

Poe's time at the University of Virginia was cut short when John Allan withdrew him in December 1826, but Poe's presence can still be felt at the school. In 1904 a group of honor students at UVA formed The Raven Society to honor Poe's association with the university. They were given West Range, number 13, to use for a shrine to Edgar Allan Poe. The room had reportedly been his dormitory room. It was renovated and opened as a museum in 1909. The room was again improved in 2011, and is maintained by the university. It features clear glass across the doorway so that visitors can look into the room to see furnishings and books like those that would have been in the room in 1826.[10]

and Other Poems printed by Calvin F. Thomas of Boston. Its author was named only as "A Bostonian." Between forty and two hundred copies were printed. The slim volume did not attract a lot of attention in 1827, and it was never publicly reviewed.[11] Its author would remain unknown for several more years.

Meanwhile, Poe continued his life as a soldier. His unit was transferred to Charleston, South Carolina, where he served as company clerk and assistant in his company's supply department. Charleston would later become the backdrop for Poe's story "The Gold Bug." According to Dr. Philip Beidler, Poe's intelligence and ability to learn new tasks made him "the kind of enlisted soldier who quickly catches the eye of unit officers."[12] On January 1, 1829, Edgar Perry was promoted to the rank of Sergeant-Major.

Soon Poe revealed his true identity to his commanding officers. At the time, a soldier could leave the army if he could find a substitute to take his place. Poe's superiors suggested that Poe ask John Allan to find a replacement and pay him to serve in Poe's place in order that Poe might leave his army unit and enroll as a cadet at West Point. This would help him advance and achieve a higher rank in the military.

About this time, Mrs. Allan became ill. Poe was given leave from his post, but arrived in Richmond the day after the funeral. Shortly after, Allan wrote to Poe's commanding officers, informing them that a substitute had been found, and asking that Poe be released. Hervey Allen suggests that Allan's gesture to help his foster-son may have been motivated by Mrs. Allan's last request that he not abandon Poe, or it simply may have been because "it seemed to offer a final solution as to his ward's future and definitely removed him from the household."[13] Poe received letters of recommendation from his army superiors, as well as an endorsement by Andrew Stevenson, Speaker of the House, in favor of his acceptance as a cadet to West Point. Poe was released from his army unit on April 15, 1829.

The Work of a "Fine Genius"

While he waited for his appointment to West Point, Poe went to Baltimore to visit relatives of his father. Poe gathered some poems he had written while he was in the army, along with a revised version of "Tamerlane", and took them to an editor in Baltimore. The editor was encouraging, and Poe soon found a publisher for a new book of poems. Hatch & Dunning, published 250 copies of the seventy-two page book, entitled *Al Aaraaf, Tamerlane, and Minor Poems*. This time, the title page included the words, "By Edgar A. Poe." A review in *Ladies' Magazine*, probably written by writer and literary critic John Neal, credited Poe with having written some poems "which remind us of no less a poet than [British poet Percy Bysshe] Shelley," although Neal dismisses others as being "exceedingly boyish." He concluded, "The author, who appears to be very young, is evidently a fine genius; but he wants judgment, experience, tact."[14] Poe was encouraged by the reception of his small volume.

He returned home to Richmond for the next few months, but his relationship with John Allan was still difficult. Allan was not supportive of Poe's ambition to write, and the two often quarreled. Allan was quite ready to send his foster son away. In March 1830, Poe received his appointment to West Point.

West Point Cadet

Poe entered West Point at the age of twenty-one, much older than most of his classmates. He was a good student, and did well at both French and mathematics. He seems to have made

Poe had a rocky relationship with his foster father, John Allan. They fought often, and it is likely that Allan resented having to financially support Poe.

friends among the other cadets, although their later stories of him indicate that he sometimes told them stories that he had sailed on a whaling ship and a merchant vessel, and that he had traveled through Egypt and Arabia.[15] His West Point roommate, Thomas W. Gibson, called Poe's knowledge of English literature "extensive and accurate," and said Poe could "repeat both prose and poetry by the hour, and seldom or never repeated the same passage twice to the same audience."[16] According to Gibson, he and Poe enjoyed playing pranks, and once convinced classmates that Gibson had murdered a professor and cut off his head. Gibson also recalled that Poe was known for his humorous verse in which he made fun of officers and fellow cadets.

While at West Point, Poe occasionally wrote to John Allan, often asking for money. Most of these requests were ignored. That fall, Allan married Louisa Patterson. He appeared to be ready to end all connections with Poe, in favor of beginning a family with his new wife. Meanwhile, Poe grew tired of the regimented life of a soldier. He asked Allan to arrange his release, but Allan did not respond. Poe stopped attending church, classes, and military drills. On January 28, 1831, a court-martial was held to try him on charges including "gross neglect of duty." He was convicted and dismissed from the academy, effective March 6, 1831.

Off to New York

Poe left West Point, bound for New York to make arrangements with publisher Elam Bliss to produce a new book of his verse. According to Thomas Gibson, the cadets at West Point heard about the new book shortly after Poe left. Thinking it would contain the humorous verses he had written at the academy, they each sent two dollars and fifty cents to receive copies. The book was entitled *Poems*, and was dedicated "To the U.S. Corps of Cadets." Evidently, the cadets were quite disappointed with the volume when it arrived a few months after Poe had left the academy. According to Gibson, "It was a puny volume . . . bound in boards and badly printed on coarse paper, and worse than all, it contained not one of the squibs and satires upon which his reputation at the Academy had been built up."[17] Despite the disappointment of the cadets, *Poems* is generally considered an important work by the talented young poet.

LAUNCHING A LITERARY CAREER

*P*oems by Edgar A. Poe appeared in print in 1831. Most of the poems in the slim volume of 124 pages had appeared in Poe's two previously published books, although some pieces had been revised in this new collection. At the age of only twenty-two, Poe was far younger than most of the notable poets of his day. English professor and Poe scholar Daniel Hoffman has said that these early poems show the immaturity of their author. "A young poet must discover who he is; he must create himself as a poet. Even a genius must do this," said Hoffman. "Poe, like any young man teaching himself to be a poet, made a couple of false starts."[1] Although many of the works in this collection are not familiar to readers today, *Poems* marks the start of Poe's career as a writer and foreshadows the poet he would become.

A New Version of *Tamerlane*

Although "Tamerlane" originally appeared in Poe's first book in 1827, the 1829 edition was revised. The version included in *Poems* had again been revised. The poem had over four hundred lines in its original version, but he trimmed the 1831 version to only 252.

Arthur Hobson Quinn calls the later version "markedly improved" and says that it shows Poe's "capacity for criticism and the striving for perfection which are two of the traits that have won him the esteem of all competent judges of poetry."[2]

"A Cheat"

One of the few existing copies of *Poems* published in 1831 belongs to the Poe Museum in Richmond, Virginia. It was purchased by one of Poe's classmates at West Point, John Pendleton Hardin. He gave it to his father Ben Hardin Jr. Evidently, Mr. Hardin was not pleased with the gift. On the first page he wrote, "This book is a damn cheat. All that fills 124 pages could be compiled in 36." To see pictures of the book, visit the Poe Museum's website (see Further Reading on p. 157).[3]

The poem tells the story of the Mongolian chief, Tamerlane, also known as Timuri Leng, a descendent of Ghengis Khan.[4] The story is not historically accurate, but Poe used the historical character to be the narrator in the poem. Poe's Tamerlane is old, and is speaking from his deathbed to a priest. Tamerlane is remembering his youth, and is regretting his decision to give up love for ambition.

Tamerlane's Themes

In this early poem, Poe introduces the major themes that appear in most of his work: pride, love, beauty, and death. The conqueror Tamerlane was tempted by his pride to pursue power and might. Although he began life as a son of a shepherd, he left this simple life to earn the fear and respect of men as well as a crown and throne. To pursue his desire for power, Tamerlane left behind the love of his youth, one whose beauty was perfection. When at last he returns to his home intending to make his lover a queen, Tamerlane finds that she has died. At the end of the poem, Tamerlane welcomes death himself.

Poe's narrator in the poem, Tamerlane, was a fourteenth-century Mongolian leader, illustrated here.

He believes that death "Hath left his iron gate ajar," so that he may go through.

Rhyme and Meter in *Tamerlane*

"Tamerlane" is not as highly structured as many of Poe's later poems would be. He divides the poems into numbered sections, but they are many different lengths, with some sections as short as four lines and others as long as twenty-two lines.

Poe's use of rhyme in "Tamerlane" is an important feature. To examine rhyme scheme in poetry, it is helpful to mark rhyming lines in a consistent way. To label rhyme scheme, letters of the alphabet are used (starting with A) to identify the end sound of each line. If the line rhymes with one before it, it will be identified with the same letter. If it has a new sound, it is given the next letter of the alphabet. Poe used different rhyme schemes in different sections of the poem. For example, in the six lines of section IV, here is the rhyme scheme:

On mountain soil I first drew life—	A
The mists of the Taglay have shed	B
Nightly their dews upon my head,	B
And I believe the winged strife	A
And tumult of the headlong air	C
Hath nestled in my very hair.[5]	C

Poe uses a different pattern in section XI, another six-line section of the poem:

We grew in age and love together,	A
Roaming the forest and the wild,	B
My breast her shield in wintry weather,	A
And, when the friendly sunshine smil'd,	B
And she would mark the opening skies,	C
I saw no Heaven—but in her eyes.[6]	C

The one constant of the poem's structure is its meter. In the language of poetry, meter is measured in "feet." A poetic foot is much like a measure in music, and consists of repeated patterns of accented and unaccented syllables. These accents come from the natural pronunciation of the words themselves and in the way they are spoken within the sentences. It should not be forced by the reader in a way that makes words sound unnatural or gives a "sing-song" tone to the poem.

> **rhyme scheme**
>
> A pattern of rhyming words at the ends of lines of a poem. These are shown by labeling words that rhyme with letters of the alphabet, beginning with A. Repeated rhymes are marked with the same letter; new sounds are marked with the next letter of the alphabet.

The meter of "Tamerlane" is based on the iamb. An iamb is a two-syllable poetic foot, with the accent on the second syllable. Each line of the poem has eight syllables, with four accented beats. Poetry in which each line has four iambs is called iambic tetrameter, using the prefix "tetra" meaning "four."

> - / - / - / - /
> And O! I have no words to tell
> - / - / - / - /
> The loveliness of loving well![7]

Although there are some minor variations, this iambic tetrameter is used throughout the poem. The rhymes and meter of the poem, together with its story of love, ambition, and loss, show Poe's abilities to combine the techniques of the poet with those of the storyteller.

Between Heaven and Hell: "Al Aaraaf"

The longest work in *Poems*, over 400 lines, is also the longest poem Poe ever published, "Al Aaraaf". It had first been published in the 1829 book *Al Aaraaf, Tamerlane, and Minor Poems*. Poe took his inspiration for the story from a "star" (actually a nova) discovered by the Danish astronomer Tycho Brahe in the 1500s. Poe combined this idea of a "wandering star" with the Middle Eastern name Al Orf, or Al Arâf, a place which is neither heaven nor hell where souls go after death.[8] In a footnote in *Poems*, Poe describes this place as follows: "a medium between Heaven and Hell, where men suffer no punishment, but yet do not attain that tranquil and even happiness which they suppose to be characteristic of heavenly enjoyment."[9]

Poe introduces this long poem with a shorter poem entitled "To Science". In this shorter verse, he says that science, in taking away the mysteries of the beauty of the universe, destroys the imagination of the poet. This idea is echoed in "Al Aaraaf." Again, Poe's themes of pride, beauty, love, and death are present.

Al Aaraaf is a place of natural beauty and exotic flowers in which angels live. Foremost among the angels is Nesace, who represents the ideal of beauty. Also in Al Aaraaf lives Angelo, who was transported there when earth was destroyed by the prideful behavior of men who created God in their own image. Nesace calls the spirits in Al Aaraaf to awaken from their dreaming and leave Al Aaraaf to travel to paradise. Angelo and his angel lover, Ianthe, resist her call, because they

---

meter

pattern of rhythm in a poem caused by the repeating patterns of stressed and unstressed syllables.

foot

A part of a line of poetry consisting of stressed and unstressed syllables. The foot is repeated to form a rhythmic pattern, such as iambic tetrameter or trochaic septameter.

do not want to give up their love of each other to be transported to be with God. Poe's note tells the reader that because they choose to stay in Al Aaraaf, they will suffer "final death and annihilation."[10]

Through the years, many critics have had difficulty understanding and appreciating "Al Aaraaf." Critic Scott Peeples calls this poem "Poe's most challenging, though hardly his most rewarding, poem."[11] He says that perhaps Poe intended "the pointlessness of 'Al Aaraaf' as the point of 'Al Aaraaf'."[12] Poe scholar Daniel Hoffman contends that the long poem is not successful. "If this be an epic," he says, "it is an epic without an epic hero; if it be legend, it is the legend of no people."[13]

The Perfection of *To Helen*

To modern readers, the love poem 'To Helen' is probably the best known selection from *Poems*. It is also one of the best of Poe's poems, according to many critics. Hoffman says that "none of [Poe's] tales speak with the memorable haunting tone of his cameo masterpiece, 'To Helen.'"[14] Literary scholar Bettina Knapp praises the poem for "bringing forth objective and impersonal images of universal beauty and artistic and technical excellence."[15] Even writer and critic Aldous Huxley, who disliked most of Poe's poetry, called this poem "perfect."[16]

Poe said that his inspiration for this poem was Mrs. Jane Craig Stanard, the mother of Robert Stanard, one of Poe's friends from the school he attended in Richmond in 1823. Mrs. Stanard

iamb(ic)

Meter made of two-syllable units (feet), consisting of an unaccented syllable, followed by an accented syllable.

tetrameter

A line of poetry containing four metric feet.

In Greek mythology, Helen of Troy was considered the most beautiful woman in the world. Poe references classical mythology as well as the idea of beauty in his poem, "To Helen."

was kind to the quiet and serious teenager, and provided a listening ear when he discussed his problems.[17] Sadly, she was very ill and died in 1824 at the age of thirty-one, when Poe was fifteen years old. Some scholars have suggested, however, that Poe's foster mother Frances Allan was actually the inspiration for the poem.[18] Although scholars have debated the identity of the human model for Helen, the beautiful woman in the poem becomes the classical ideal of beauty, Helen of Troy.

The version included in *Poems* in 1831 is slightly different from the poem most people are familiar with today. Poe made some changes over the years, including the rewording of lines nine and ten, the most-quoted phrases of the poem. Here is the poem with its usual wording, marked with meter and rhyme scheme:

/ - - / - / - /
Helen, thy beauty is to me   A
    /   - - / - / - /
    Like those Nicean barks of yore,   B
- / - / - / - /
That gently, o'er a perfumed sea,   A
    - / - / - / - /
    The weary way-worn wanderer bore   B
    - / - / - /
    To his own native shore.   B

- / -- / - / - /
On desperate seas long wont to roam,   C
    - / -- / - / - /
    Thy hyacinth hair, thy classic face,   D
- / - / - / - /
Thy Naiad airs have brought me home   C

```
  -   -  /  -    -    -    /
```
To the glory that was Greece,   D
```
  -    -      /    -    -    -    /
```
And the grandeur that was Rome.   C
```
  /   -   -   /   -   /   -   /
```
Lo ! in yon brilliant window-niche   E
```
    -   /  -   /  -  /   -   /
```
How statue-like I see thee stand,   F
```
  -  /  -   /   -  /   -   /
```
The agate lamp within thy hand!   F
```
    -    /   -   /   -   /   -    /
```
Ah, Psyche, from the regions which   E
```
  -  /  -   /
```
Are Holy land![19]   F

The poet compares Helen's beauty to the boats ("barks") of Nicea (an ancient city, now known as Iznik, located in Turkey). In the poem, these boats brought warriors back to their homes in ancient Greece and Rome. He compares her hair to the hyacinth, a flower native to Greece, and her "airs," or demeanor, to that of the naiads, beautiful nymphs of Greek mythology. At the end of the poem he compares her to the beautiful princess Psyche of Roman mythology, who loved Cupid, the god of love. Agate, a semi-translucent stone, was valued as a gemstone in ancient Greece, as well as today. Many poets of Poe's era regarded the ancient world as the birthplace of the greatest art, music, poetry, and philosophy. He is saying that Helen's beauty is able to transport his imagination back to those times of greatness.

Musical Qualities of "To Helen"

This poem of Poe's youth displays the types of musical qualities for which he would later become famous. As shown in the marked version of the poem above, Poe has certainly used rhyme in the poem, but he has not repeated the same rhyme patterns in the three separate parts, or stanzas, of the poem. He also uses an approximate rhyme in line nine, since "Greece" does not exactly rhyme with "face." Because the lines of "To Helen" are fairly short, a predictable rhyme scheme could have given the poem a nursery rhyme sound or "sing-song" effect. Instead, Poe's irregular rhyme scheme makes the rhyme easy to hear, but difficult to predict, and helps it keep a more serious tone.

The meter of the poem is also irregular. In the first and third stanzas, the first four lines of the stanza each have four beats, and are generally in iambic tetrameter, although the rhythm varies slightly in some lines. The last line of each of these stanzas is shorter, however. The middle stanza is different from the others because lines nine and ten are similar to each other, but are not in iambic tetrameter. They each have seven syllables. As with the irregular rhyme, this variation in meter helps to empha-size the meaning of the poem over the sound of it. Poe's use of these poetic techniques showed his talent for producing meaningful, yet musical poetry at a young age. Quinn says it "is pure pleasure in the exquisite harmony of the phrases, creating that unity in variety that makes for great art."[20]

---

stanza

A section of a poem that is separated from other parts.

Classical Themes in "To Helen"

Poe's love poem does not include all of the themes commonly found in many of his other works. It certainly contains the ideas of both ideal beauty and love, but it does not include the prideful defeat of its speaker. It also does not involve the death of Helen. The only suggestion of death could possibly be the

Some scholars believe that Poe's foster mother, Frances Allan, was the real-life inspiration for "To Helen."

reference to the bygone civilizations of ancient Greece and Rome. Poe probably did not write "To Helen" when he was a teenager, since he did not include it in either of his two earlier books of poetry. Still, as Quinn points out, the memory of Mrs. Stanard may have reminded him of that time in his youth when he was probably studying the works of the Greek author Homer and the Roman author Cicero in school.[21]

The poem explores the similarity between a real journey and a journey of the spirit and imagination. The opening stanza speaks of ships on the sea that take travelers both away from home and then back again. After these travels, it is the memory of Helen's beauty that brings the poet back home. In the final stanza, he sees her standing in a window, holding a lamp to guide him.

On a symbolic level, the poet's journey is one that occurs in his imagination. Helen is not a living woman, but the memory or vision of ideal beauty. From Roman mythology, Psyche is seen as a symbol of the human soul. Poe's reference to Psyche in line fourteen suggests that this is not a physical journey, but one of the spirit. Helen has provided the poet's inspiration that allows him to escape the physical world and enter the world of the ideal. As critic Scott Peeples puts it, "her beauty, whether seen in the flesh or imagined by the poet, leads him to his poetic home, the 'glory' and 'grandeur' of those 'holy lands' of poetry and art."[22]

Many scholars consider "To Helen" to be among the finest of Poe's poems. Vincent Buranelli compared the work to that of the French Parnassian (a style of poetry that emphasized precision and perfection) poets of the nineteenth century, who "made it their ideal to write just so."[23] Critic John Neal reviewed *Poems* in July 1831 in both the *Morning Courier* and the *New York Enquirer*. He quoted lines from "To Helen" because he believed it illustrated "Pure Poetry" and showed that "the author has the gift." Although he did criticize some of the other verses in the book as being "sheer nonsense," he acknowledged that Poe "is evidently a fellow of fine genius."[24] The poem's success was Poe's first step toward being considered a man of letters.

AUTHOR, CRITIC, EDITOR

At age twenty-two, Poe's literary career was just beginning, but he could not yet support himself with his writing. After the publication of *Poems*, he left New York and moved in with his father's sister, Maria Clemm, in Baltimore. His older brother, William Henry, also lived with Mrs. Clemm and her two children: a boy named Henry and a girl named Virginia. Poe's grandmother lived there as well. It was the first time Poe had lived with blood relatives since his mother's death.

Mrs. Clemm was very motherly toward Poe, and he affectionately called her "Muddy." He referred to Virginia as "Sissy." The family lived on his grandmother's pension, and Poe spent his time reading books of science and philosophy. He also turned his attention from writing poetry to stories at this time. He wrote several stories for a contest sponsored by the Philadelphia *Saturday Courier*. He did not win the contest, but the stories were published in the magazine without his name.

Poe's brother William died in August 1831. When his cousin Henry left home to go to sea, Poe was left with his grandmother, Maria Clemm, and Virginia. According to accounts of acquaintances, he applied himself to his writing while in Baltimore and apparently stayed away from strong drink.[1]

In the early 1830s, Poe lived in this small Baltimore house with his aunt, grandmother, and two young cousins.

More Writing Work

In 1833, Poe sent several stories handwritten in a small book entitled *Tales of the Folio Club,* to a new magazine, *The Baltimore Saturday Visiter* [sic], in response to a contest. The story "Ms. Found in a Bottle", (Ms is often used as shorthand for manuscript in literary circles) received the first prize of fifty dollars. A poem Poe had submitted, "The Coliseum", was also chosen for the poetry contest, but since it was submitted by the same author as the story, the committee gave the poetry prize to another writer. "Ms. Found in a Bottle" by Edgar Allan Poe was published in the magazine.

Poe submitted stories to several magazines, and also did some newspaper writing, although his name was never attached to any of these items. He continued to write stories, and submitted some to Thomas W. White, editor of the *Southern Literary Messenger.* White liked Poe's writing, and asked if he would be willing to write book reviews for the magazine. Poe agreed, but White would only pay him a small amount for each piece. Poe's book reviews began receiving attention. At last he was receiving some recognition within the literary community, but he was still not making enough money to support himself and his extended family.

Poe appealed to John Allan for help, and Allan did respond with some money, but Poe needed steady employment. By January of 1834 John Allan's second wife, Louisa, had given birth to three children. Allan also had illegitimate children for which he admitted responsibility. In March 1834, Allan died, leaving Poe out of his will. When Poe's grandmother died in 1835, her pension ceased, and Poe, Maria Clemm, and Virginia were in desperate need. Poe asked White for a job, and White hired him as his assistant at the *Messenger,* at a salary of ten dollars a week.[2] By this time, Poe had written sixteen stories, and eleven of them had been published.[3]

The Sharp-Tongued Critic

The new job required Poe to move from Baltimore to Richmond in the summer of 1835. Through his new position he was able to publish some of his previous work, and to re-publish a few stories that had already appeared in print. He did very little new creative work, however, because White employed him in a new role: literary critic.[4]

Poe immediately gained attention for himself and for the *Messenger*. His reviews brought the *Messenger* to the notice of readers of more famous and well-read literary publications like *The Knickerbocker* and *The New Englander*. American critics, in their desire to support American authors, often praised poor writing. In an article in the *Messenger* in 1836, Poe objected to this practice of "liking a stupid book the better because, sure enough, its stupidity is American."[5] Poe was witty, sharp, and sometimes brutal in his appraisals of popular novelists and poets. At the age of only twenty-five, he soon gained the attention of the literary community, although they did not always like what he had to say. According to biographer George Woodberry, "What distinguished Poe was the audacity with which he took the unenvied post, and the vigor with which he struck."[6]

Most of the popular American literature of the day was coming out of the New England states, and the New England literary community considered itself superior to that in the South. While entertaining to readers, Poe's sharp-tongued reviews angered some writers, and made him enemies in the literary community, especially in New England. Still, he helped the *Messenger* grow from a circulation of 500 copies to 3500 copies per month during his time there, and his salary grew from $520 per year to nearly $800, a sum which he described in a letter to a friend as "very liberal." In this letter he says that he is "in every respect, comfortable and happy."[7]

In May 1836, Poe acquired a marriage license and found a minister to conduct a ceremony in which he married his first cousin, Virginia Clemm. Although a witness testified that Virginia was twenty-one years old, she was in fact only thirteen. Poe was twenty-seven. Their relationship as cousins has been less important to biographers than Virginia's tender age. Many have questioned their sexual relationship as a married couple, but a letter Poe wrote to Mrs. Clemm in August 1835 clearly shows the depth of his feeling for Virginia: "I love, *you know* I love Virginia passionately devotedly."[8] Still, they may not have consummated the marriage immediately. Although the couple took a honeymoon trip to Petersburg, Virginia, after the ceremony, one acquaintance whom biographer Jeffrey Meyers describes as "reliable" said that Poe and Virginia slept in separate bedrooms for the first two years of their marriage.[9]

By the fall of 1836, things were not going well at the *Messenger*. Poe wished to have more editorial power at the magazine, but White did not want to give up control. In a letter to his friend, Lucian Minor, White complained that Poe had too much power at the magazine. "I am cramped by him in the exercise of my own judgment, as to what articles I shall or shall not admit into my work."[10] Poe was also trying to have some of his own stories published, but was not having much success. It was evidently a time of great frustration for him. It took a toll on him physically, and he began drinking again. In a letter to a friend in 1841, Poe talked about this period during his work at the *Messenger*: "In short, it sometimes happened that I was completely intoxicated. For some days after each

Poe married his cousin Virginia in 1836. Marrying one's cousin was not unusual then, and even the fact that she was thirteen was not shocking for that time period.

excess I was invariably confined to bed."[11] In January 1837, White fired Poe.

The Narrative of Arthur Gordon Pym

In February, Poe moved with his wife and mother-in-law to New York. There he was successful in publishing two stories from the Folio Club collection, but little else is known of his brief time in New York. Poe did not have any significant income from his writing, nor did he have a salaried position. The economic downturn of 1837 may have contributed to Poe's inability to find a job. Mrs. Clemm took in boarders to help make ends meet, and according to William Gowans, who stayed with the family, Poe was busy with writing and was not drinking during this time.[12]

Poe did sell a longer tale, *The Narrative of Arthur Gordon Pym of Nantucket,* to Harper and Brothers Publishers in 1837. The previous year Poe had submitted a group of short stories to Harper Brothers to be published together in a book, but the publisher had rejected the idea because the stories had all been published previously, and also the editors believed that readers preferred book-length stories over collections of shorter works.[13] The beginning of the story appeared in the *Messenger* in early 1837, but Poe discontinued it after the second installment. Harper Brothers purchased the story in June 1837, and published it during the summer of 1838.

In the story, the novel's narrator, Pym, stows away on a whaling vessel bound for the South Pole. The series of fantastic events includes mutiny, murder, and even cannibalism. Pym's narration ends suddenly with the description of an enormous hole in the sea at the South Pole, and the appearance of a mysterious figure shrouded in white. A note at the end indicates that Pym is dead, and the end of his story is lost. The preface of the book describes it as a true story that Pym told Poe. Of course, Poe's novel is entirely fictitious, but some reviewers, such as the critic at *Burton's Gentleman's Magazine*, took the preface too seriously and treated it as though it were nonfiction. Because the end of the book is so imaginative, these reviewers criticized the book as a hoax. Others who reviewed the book more favorably, were confused by the fact that Poe's name was not on the title page of the book, and only mentioned in the preface. The New York *Gazette* reviewer commented, "It is hinted that Mr. Poe, the accomplished Virginia writer, has something to do about the book."[14] It did not sell well, although it was reprinted in England in a pirated version for which Poe received no pay.

Success in Philadelphia

During the summer of 1838, Poe moved with Virginia and Mrs. Clemm to Philadelphia, hopeful that he might be able to find steady work there. He wrote some articles, stories, and poems for a Baltimore magazine, *The American Museum*. Among the items published were his short story, "Ligeia," and a poem called "The Haunted Palace." He probably received between five and ten dollars for each piece published in the magazine.[15] He worked with a neighbor, Professor Thomas Wyatt, on a school textbook entitled *The Conchologist's First Book*, a textbook about sea animals and shells. Wyatt had previously written a book on the same subject, but hoped that a book with Poe's name would sell better. Poe wrote the preface and introduction to the book, and received fifty dollars from Wyatt for his help. His name appeared as the author of the book.[16]

In the spring of 1839, Poe at last was offered steady employment. He applied to work as an editor at *Burton's Gentleman's Magazine*. William Burton hired him at a salary of ten dollars

This eerie illustration of a skeleton on a ship accompanied one edition of Poe's only novel, *The Narrative of Arthur Gordon Pym of Nantucket.*

per week. The June issue of the magazine listed Edgar A. Poe as assistant editor. It marked the beginning of a period of great productivity for Poe. He wrote reviews of contemporary writers like Washington Irving and Henry Wadsworth Longfellow. He also wrote articles on subjects like gymnastic equipment, housekeeping, and Stonehenge.

Poe was able to increase his pay from Burton by contributing fiction stories and poems to the magazine. During this period, he wrote some of his most famous tales. Both "The Fall of the House of Usher" and "William Wilson" appeared in *Burton's*. Poe had previously failed to interest a publisher in his *Tales of the Folio Club*. Harper and Brothers Publishers had objected on the grounds that most of the tales had already been published in magazines.[17] Poe's new tales, however, were being praised by reviewers in New York, Philadelphia, and other cities.[18] Poe approached publishers Lea and Blanchard of Philadelphia about publishing a collection of stories. They feared that the book would not bring them a profit, but agreed to publish twenty-five stories in a two-volume set, on the condition that Poe's only payment would be some copies of the books for himself. Poe would keep the copyright on the material, an important consideration for him, in the case that he might have the opportunity to publish the stories again later. Lea and Blanchard would keep any profits from the sales of the books. Poe agreed to the terms, and *Tales of the Grotesque and Arabesque* was released near the end of the year 1839, although its title page shows a date of 1840.[19]

Poe's Premiere: Tales of the Grotesque and Arabesque

In this collection, Poe's "grotesque" stories are satires and parodies of popular literature of the day. Few of these are familiar to today's readers. The "arabesques," however, are the dark fantasy for which Poe is most known. "Ligeia," "Morella," and "The Fall of the House of Usher," all tales of the supernatural and of life after death, are among the stories that thrill Poe fans today. In the preface to *Tales of the Grotesque and Arabesque*, Poe says that in these tales "terror has been the thesis" and it is terror "of the soul."[1]

Some readers were disturbed by the tales of death and the supernatural and the ghastly images Poe described in them. Others did not like the disrespect that Poe displayed in some of the tales that satirized some of the notable authors of the day. The reviewer of the *Boston Morning Post* commented, "A greater amount of trash . . . would be difficult to find."[2]

Other magazines, however, gave much more favorable reviews. Louis F. Tasistro of the *New York Mirror* praised the book and its author, claiming that Poe "would deserve a high place among imaginative writers," and that the stories all showed "the development of great intellectual capacity."[3] And *Alexander's Weekly Messenger* carried a review that said Poe "is

This photo of Poe was taken around the time that *Tales of the Grotesque and Arabesque* came out.

capable of great things," and "has placed himself in the fore-most rank of American writers."[4]

Examining *The Fall of the House of Usher*

Probably the most notable tale of the collection, and the one most familiar to modern readers, is "The Fall of the House of Usher." Poe scholar Vincent Buranelli calls it "perhaps the finest thing Poe ever wrote."[5]

The story begins with our narrator, who is never named, approaching the home of his friend Roderick Usher. The narrator learns that Roderick and his sister Madeline are the last remaining members of their family. Roderick says that his sister is dying, and that he is suffering from a peculiar illness himself. Over the next few days, Roderick grows more ill, and his sister dies. The narrator helps Roderick close Madeline in a casket and seal it in a tomb deep within the house.

As days pass, Roderick becomes more and more distracted, and seems to be slipping into insanity. In the final scene of the story, a fierce storm comes up. To calm his friend, the narrator reads a story to him, but they begin hearing strange sounds coming from deep in the house. Roderick says that he has been hearing the sounds for days, and now realizes that Madeline was not really dead when they put her in the tomb. They open the door, and Madeline enters, dressed in her burial clothes and covered with blood. She falls onto her brother, and both of them sink to the floor, dead. The narrator rushes from the house into the raging storm and turns to see the house collapse behind him.

Narrative Techniques in Usher

In this story, Poe uses many of the techniques he would continue to use in stories throughout his career. In 1842 Poe wrote a review of Nathaniel Hawthorne's book *Twice Told Tales* for *Graham's Magazine*, and in his review, Poe presented his ideas about good fiction. Although the review was published over two years after "The Fall of the House of Usher," Poe's ideas relating to writing were clearly present in this story.

Poe believed writers should strive for "unity of effect." This means that, once the author has determined the effect he wants to create for the reader, he must then be sure that everything in the story, beginning with the first word, contributes to this effect. "If his very initial sentence tend not to the outbringing of this effect, then he has failed in his first step,"[6] he said. Poe sets the gloomy and dark mood of Usher in its very first sentence:

> During the hole of a dull, dark, and soundless day in the autumn of the year, when the clouds hung oppressively low in the heavens, I had been passing alone, on horseback, through a singularly dreary tract of country; and at length found myself, as the shades of evening drew on, within view of the melancholy House of Usher.[7]

The detailed description continues throughout the story, so that the reader can visualize the dark lake that surrounds the house, the gloomy, candlelit interior of the mansion, and hear the mournful songs Roderick plays on his guitar.

Another device Poe uses in "The Fall of the House of Usher" is the first-person point of view. Most of the stories in *Tales of the Grotesque and Arabesque* are told this way, from the point of view and in the voice of a character within the story. This narrator calls himself "I," and relates the events of the story as he has seen or experienced them. Poe's use of the first-person narrator creates an immediate connection between the reader and the narrator. From the beginning of the story, the reader listens directly to the narrator and "hears" his voice. As the story continues, the reader may even begin to identify with the narrator, so that each time he or she reads the word "I," it seems like the reader is placed within the person of the narrator and is experiencing the story along with him. As our narrator describes the effect that the gloomy setting has on his mind, the reader can begin to feel it, too. When the narrator runs from the house as it collapses behind him, the reader may also feel that he or she has just made a narrow escape.

Poe also uses symbolism in the story. Unlike some authors who require readers to pick up subtle suggestions in order to understand the symbolism, Poe tells us early on that the name "House of Usher" applies to "both the family and the family mansion." The narrator speaks of a crack in the house that extends from just below the roof all the way down to its foundation, a suggestion that the house may soon fall. We soon learn that Roderick and Madeline are the last in their family, and both of them will probably die soon. In other words, both the house itself and the family will be destroyed.

Poe continues this technique of doubles in other areas of the story as well. As our narrator approaches the house, he is aware of its image as it is reflected in the dark lake that surrounds it, the tarn. When he sees Madeline, our narrator is surprised at the resemblance between Roderick and his sister. He learns that they are twins. Again, a double image. They are nearly identical, but opposite, male and female. Later, Poe suggests a similar relationship between sanity and insanity; although they are opposite, they may be so alike that it is hard to tell one from the other. These techniques have led readers to many different interpretations of the story through the years.

THE FALL OF THE HOUSE OF USHER

The climax of "The Fall of the House of Usher" occurs when Roderick's sister appears from the tomb, bloodied and dressed in white.

Interpretations of "Usher"

"The Fall of the House of Usher" is both simple and complex at the same time. Taken just as a horror story, it offers an imaginative and exciting plot filled with images that come to life for the reader. Beyond this, however, Poe has built many elements into the story that invite readers to read for deeper meaning. Critics for years have debated alternate interpretations of the story. They have approached the story from symbolic, scientific, and psychological viewpoints.

Many of the stories in *Tales of the Grotesque and Arabesque* include the same themes Poe used in other works: love, pride, beauty, and death. In "Usher" as well as many of the other stories, the death of a beautiful woman is an important part of the story. Several of the stories, including "Ligeia," "Morella," and "Bernice," also dwell on a new idea: return from death, or in this case, from apparent death. Poe would continue to use this element in his stories.

Poe also explores in many of his stories the fine line between sanity and insanity. Roderick's literary collection and musical talent show that he is a man of great intelligence. Soon after our narrator's arrival, however, he expresses the fear that he is going mad. As his sister becomes weaker, Roderick's mental state weakens as well. Continuing his use of doubles in the story, Poe presents Roderick's song of the "Haunted Palace," a poem with a double meaning.

Roderick describes a beautiful palace with yellow banners on the roof, luminous windows, and a door of pearl and ruby. In the fifth line, he introduces the double meaning of the poem as he tells us the king of this land was "Thought." Contrasted to the narrator's earlier description of the Usher house with its "vacant, eye-like windows," we can apply the description of the palace to a person. By comparison, this palace is like a person's head, with flowing blonde hair, sparkling eyes, and lips and teeth showing a smile in the "happy valley" of clear thoughts. After the "evil things in robes of sorrow" invade the palace, it completely changes. Now the eyes are lit with red, the thoughts "move fantastically to a discordant melody," and hysterical but joyless laughter escapes through the door.

Of course, this is exactly what our narrator sees happening to Roderick. After Madeline's death, Roderick slips deeper and deeper into insanity. According to Scott Peeples, "the song creates a precise parallel between house and man of the house," and provides us "a miniature double of the tale itself."[8]

Other critics believe that this is the story of the narrator's own insanity. Poe suggests this at the climax of the story when Roderick calls the narrator "Madman!" Professor John S. Hill points to the narrator's comment on the effect of Roderick's madness upon his own mind: "I felt creeping upon me, by slow yet certain degrees, the wild influences of his own fantastic yet impressive superstitions." He believes that Madeline's appearance at the end of the story is a shared hallucination of Roderick and the narrator.

Logically, if Madeline were so weak as to have appeared to be dead, she could not possibly have escaped the screwed-on lid of the coffin or opened the heavy metal door of the chamber, after having been in the chamber without food for a week. According to Hill, "[The narrator] does not realize that Madeline is an apparition, for by the end of the story he is insane enough to conjure a hallucination too."[9]

Some critics believe that Roderick also exists only in the narrator's imagination. Poet and critic Richard Wilbur says the story is "a dream of the narrator's, in which he leaves behind him the waking, physical world and journeys inward toward his inner and spiritual self. That inner and spiritual self is Roderick Usher."[10] Critic Clark Griffith says similarly, "The Ushers are the products of the narrator's psyche; for they and their behavior become the embodiments of his trance."[11]

The narrator's descriptions of the dark lake, the tarn, next to the house may even suggest a physical cause of insanity. Professor I. M. Walker quotes a scientific article published shortly before Poe published "Usher" that presented the idea that vapors called "miasma," rising from foul water could affect the mind and cause insanity and hallucinations.[12]

Still others have attempted to interpret the story with the help of theories of psychology. Writer D. H. Lawrence viewed the story through the theory of Swiss psychiatrist Carl Jung, and concluded that the central problem of the story is an incestuous relationship between Roderick and Madeline.[13]

Psychoanalyst Louise J. Kaplan interprets the story as one of denied physical incest, but suggests that the final scene of the story represents the spiritual merging of Roderick and Madeline, the ultimate act of incest.[14]

These many different ways of interpreting the story demonstrate that there is no single "correct" way of understanding it. Each reader may consider the story differently. We can never be sure if Poe intended the tale to be a story of the supernatural, a psychological thriller, or perhaps both. Critic G. R. Thompson says that Poe denies "the ability of the human mind ever to know anything with certainty; whether about the external reality of the world or about the internal reality of the mind."[15]

Success and Failure of *Tales*

Despite the favorable reviews it received, the book did not sell well. In 1841 Poe asked Lea and Blanchard to produce a second

Poe's short story "Ligeia" was first published in 1838, then reprinted two years later in *Tales of the Grotesque and Arabesque*. The story deals with the death of the narrator's two wives, with the second wife ultimately coming back from the dead as the first wife. This illustration depicts the scene in which the narrator first sees Ligeia.

MUSICAL POE

In 1976 the rock band Alan Parsons Project released its first album, entitled *Tales of Mystery and Imagination*. The songs on the album are all inspired by the works of Edgar Allan Poe. Tracks include "The Raven," "The Cask of Amontillado," "The Fall of the House of Usher," and more. The unique combination of instruments like organ, synthesizer, and glockenspiel give the music an eerie mood. A web search with the phrase "Edgar Allan Poe Alan Parsons Project" will yield several YouTube links to music videos of the album.

edition of *Tales of the Grotesque and Arabesque*, to which he would contribute eight new tales.[16] They declined Poe's offer, saying, "As yet we have not got through the edition of the other work & up to this time it has not returned to us the expense of its publication."[17] Fortunately, Poe's reputation as a writer did not depend upon the number of books sold. The tales had already gained a wide readership for Poe through their publication in the various magazines to which Poe contributed. Poe would soon achieve national recognition as a poet, writer, and editor.

THE STRUGGLING WRITER

The next few years brought some encouragement for the young writer, but also struggles and heartache. In 1839 and 1840, he continued his work at *Burton's Gentleman's Magazine*, and also wrote for *Alexander's Weekly Messenger*. Besides writing regular articles for the newspaper, Poe also started a puzzle series. He called the puzzles "ciphers," and they became instantly popular with readers.

Each cipher presented a message in a code created by substituting one letter of the alphabet for another, such as replacing each A in the message with a G, and each B with an H, etc. Poe invited readers to send in their own coded messages for him to solve, and he published these codes and his solutions in the newspaper. *Alexander's Weekly Messenger* ran the series for several months.[1]

Through the spring of 1840, Poe continued to work for *Burton's* in his role as editor, but contributed very few new stories or poems of his own. He contributed only one short story, "Peter Pendulum the Business Man", and one poem, "Sonnet—Silence", which had earlier been published in the *Philadelphia Saturday Courier*. By May 1840, Burton was having financial difficulties and had stopped paying contributors. Poe's last contributions to William Burton for the magazine appeared in the June 1840 issue. Poe was not sorry to leave *Burton's*. He wanted to break away from working for others as an editor and start a new magazine of his own. According to

Quinn, "On the whole, his association with *Burton's* had been an interruption to his creative work, made necessary by the earning of a living."[2]

It was very difficult in the mid-1800s for any writer to make a living from writing alone. The lack of international copyright laws allowed publishers in the United States to copy books published in England and sell them without paying anything to the author. Therefore, they did not want to pay an American author for stories or poems when they could copy proven best-sellers from Dickens or other foreign authors.[3] Poe hoped that publishing his own magazine would at last bring him some financial reward for his talents.

The Penn Magazine

Poe had no money to invest in his new literary venture, *The Penn Magazine.* He took ads in local papers to find subscribers and wrote letters to prominent men in Philadelphia and other cities to gain support. He planned that the first issue would appear in January 1841. Near the end of the year, progress on *Penn* was not going well for Poe. He postponed the proposed date of the first issue to March.

George R. Graham, the publisher of the magazine *Atkinson's Casket,* purchased *Burton's* in October 1840. At the beginning of 1841, Graham merged *Burton's* and the *Casket* into one magazine under the name *Graham's Magazine,* and offered Poe the job of editor. In February 1841, a banking panic sparked a financial depression, and any hope of finding investors for *Penn* evaporated.

Poe accepted Graham's offer, and began his new job at a salary of $800 per year, plus additional payment for poems and stories that he contributed to the magazine. A remark he made to his friend Joseph Evans Snodgrass in a letter indicates that

George Graham started *Graham's Magazine* in 1841. The publication was a great success, featuring the works of prominent writers like Henry Wadsworth Longfellow and James Fenimore Cooper. In addition to being an editor at the magazine, Poe also contributed a great deal of his own writing.

he considered this new job a temporary postponement in his plans: "... Mr. Graham has made me a liberal offer, which I had great pleasure in accepting. The *Penn* project will unquestionably be resumed hereafter."[4]

Poe now entered into one of the most creative and productive phases of his writing life. The April edition of *Graham's* carried a story of a new type from Poe: a tale of "ratiocination," a mystery solved by logic. "The Murders in the Rue Morgue" featured the character C. Auguste Dupin. Earlier mystery writers had used plots in which they attempted to confuse readers by first introducing misleading information, then allowing the investigator to correctly guess the real solution to the case. Instead, Dupin solves the mystery by tying together a series of clues and using deduction to arrive at a solution. Readers enjoyed the character of Dupin, and Poe would bring him back in later stories.

Poe was contributing literary reviews to *Graham's*, much as he did at the *Southern Literary Messenger*. He also helped Graham approach other authors for contributions of their writing. Well-known authors like Henry Wadsworth Longfellow and James Fennimore Cooper sent new works to Graham, and he paid them well: $50 for a poem by Longfellow, $1800 for a story by Cooper.[5] Meanwhile, Graham gave Poe a small amount per page for his stories and poems.

Virginia Poe

Despite their financial struggles, Poe and Virginia seemed to be completely devoted to each other. According to Poe's biographer Quinn, "As [Virginia] matured, the adoration of the child he had married grew into the devotion of the woman, and the physical attraction for the handsome young cousin she worshipped blossomed into a spiritual passion which his love had nurtured."[6]

Visitors to the home were enchanted by her grace and beauty. She entertained guests by singing and playing the piano. In January of 1842, while singing to friends in their house, Virginia suffered a broken blood vessel that caused her to clutch her throat as blood gushed from her mouth. Poe went for a doctor, but there was little he could do. This episode was the first sign of a serious illness: tuberculosis. She would seem to recover only to relapse many times in the next few years.

When Poe joined *Graham's* in 1841, Graham had suggested that, if the new magazine was successful, he would help Poe get started with *Penn Magazine*, or would give him part owner-ship of *Graham's*. By the spring of 1842, neither had happened. *Graham's* had grown quite profitable under Poe's editorship. The number of subscribers had grown from five thousand to nearly forty thousand in the first year.[7] Graham had no desire to give away part interest in the magazine. Poe began to realize that the longer he stayed at *Graham's*, the harder it would be to break away to publish *Penn*. The strain of worry about finances, his wife's health, and his dissatisfaction with his job took a toll on Poe. He began to drink again. Later, he described the despair he went through at this time in a letter to a friend:

> "[My] wife, whom I loved as no man ever loved before, ruptured a blood vessel in singing. Her life was despaired of. . . . I became insane, with long intervals of horrible sanity. During these fits of absolute unconsciousness, I drank—God only knows how often or how much. As a matter of course, my enemies referred the insanity to the drink, rather than the drink to the insanity."[8]

Poe's unreliability on the job made it difficult for Graham to keep him. No clear record exists of whether Poe was fired or quit. Poe told a friend he was tired of the love stories and fashion plates the magazine carried. In a letter he said, "My reason for resigning was disgust with the namby-pamby character of the Magazine . . . The salary, moreover, did not pay me for the labor which I was forced to bestow."[9] When Poe left *Graham's* on April 1, 1842, he had two stories already in production for the magazine, "Life in Death" (later renamed "The Oval Portrait") and "The Masque of the Red Death." He maintained a cordial relationship with George Graham, and would continue to contribute stories, poems, and reviews to *Graham's* every year for the rest of his life.

The Poes lived in Philadelphia in the early 1840s. This photograph shows the parlor of the Poe home on North Seventh Street, where Edgar and Virginia would entertain guests.

After leaving his job at *Graham's*, Poe had no way to support his sick wife and her mother. He continued to write stories, including a new tale with his now-famous detective, C. Auguste Dupin. The story, "The Mystery of Marie Roget," although set in France, was Poe's fictionalization of the mysterious murder of Mary Rogers, a tobacco store clerk in New York. Rogers' body was found in the Hudson River in August 1841, and the police had been unable to solve the case. Poe's story was purchased by the *Ladies Companion*, but would not appear until later in the year.

Poe's Despair

In the meantime, Poe went to New York hoping to find a steady job and also a publisher for a new collection of his tales. He proposed a two-volume set entitled *Phantasy-Pieces*, which would contain the twenty-five tales that had previously appeared in *Tale of the Grotesque and Arabesque*, plus eleven tales written since 1839, including "Masque of the Red Death", and "Life in Death". Poe's activities in New York between June 24 and June 27 are not clear, but according to letters and accounts of people who saw him, he evidently met poet William Ross Wallace there, and the two began drinking. Poe visited the offices of publishers while he was intoxicated. Not surprisingly, Poe found neither a job nor a publisher on the trip. Later, he would write to J. and H. G. Langley of the *Democratic Review*, "Will you be kind enough to put the best possible interpretation upon my behavior while in N-York? You must have conceived a queer idea of me—but the simple truth is that Wallace would insist upon the [drinks], and I knew not what I was either doing or saying."[10]

During this period, Virginia sometimes recovered a bit, only to relapse again. Each time she recovered, Poe was encouraged that she would live, but each time she relapsed, he fell into despair. In the meantime, the family was still struggling financially. Poe was again trying to get *Penn Magazine* started, but still had little luck finding investors.

Late that year, Poe submitted a new story, "The Tell-Tale Heart," to *Boston Miscellany*, but it was rejected. He was encouraged, however, by poet James Russell Lowell, who was just beginning a new magazine, *The Pioneer*. Lowell purchased the story for the first issue. Poe had made his mark as a great storyteller, but he had achieved neither financial success nor the recognition of the literary community.

Storyteller and Lecturer

The year 1843 began on a good note for Poe. "The Tell-Tale Heart" appeared in *The Pioneer*; *Graham's* carried Poe's poem, "The Conqueror Worm"; and "The Mystery of Marie Roget" was still running in the *Ladies Companion*. Best of all, Poe had finally found a backer for his magazine. Thomas C. Clarke, owner of *The Saturday Museum*, a weekly Philadelphia newspaper, signed an agreement with Poe to publish the first issue of the new magazine on July 1. They renamed it *The Stylus*. Their plan did not materialize. In May, Clarke withdrew his offer to finance the publishing of *The Stylus*, probably because of financial difficulty with his newspaper.

Despite his disappointment, Poe continued writing. He submitted a new story, entitled "The Gold Bug," to a contest sponsored by the *Dollar Newspaper*. The tale included hidden pirate treasure found by breaking a coded message, similar to the "ciphers" he had published years earlier in *Alexander's Weekly Messenger*. Poe won the contest and was awarded one hundred dollars for the story. It became so popular with readers that it was even turned into a stage play.

The remainder of the year included other successes for Poe. William H. Graham published a pamphlet entitled "Prose Romances" that contained Poe's "Murders in the Rue Morgue" and "The Man That was Used Up." In August, another new story, "The Black Cat," appeared in the *Saturday Evening Post*. Public lectures were popular entertainment in this era, and many authors made more money from the tickets sold to their lectures than they did from writing. In the fall, Poe delivered a lecture in Philadelphia to a crowd that overflowed the auditorium, and many people were turned away.[11]

Over the next few months Poe delivered several such lectures, most on the subject of "American Poetry." Audiences enjoyed Poe's often sharp and witty comments on the poets of the day. On stage, Poe became especially critical of Rufus W. Griswold, the editor who had replaced him at Graham's. Poe ridiculed Griswold's book, *Poets and Poetry of America,* in his lectures. Naturally, reviewers commented on Poe's remarks, and Griswold learned of Poe's repeated public mockery of him. Over the next few years, the relationship between the two men would be sometimes cordial, sometimes not.

A New Job and a Breakthrough

In April 1844, Poe moved to New York with Virginia and Mrs. Clemm, hoping to find new writing opportunities. For six months the family moved from one place to another, usually because they were unable to pay the rent.[12] In October, Nathaniel Willis, editor of the New York *Evening Mirror* newspaper, offered Poe a position as assistant editor for a yearly salary of $750. Although it was less than he had made years before at *Graham's*, it was steady employment. In addition to the pieces he contributed to the *Mirror*, Poe continued to work on other stories, returning to his famous character Dupin for

"The Murders in the Rue Morgue" was first published in *Graham's Magazine* in 1841. It is considered by many to be the first modern detective story. This illustration shows the murder scene, in which an orangutan attacks a woman and her daughter.

yet one more detective story, "The Purloined Letter." He also wrote "The Premature Burial," "The Balloon-Hoax," and "A Tale of the Ragged Mountains" for publication in 1844.

Poe's biggest breakthrough in his writing career came with the publication of "The Raven" in January 1845. Although he had been writing many stories, Poe had written few poems in the previous decade. In his literary criticism, Poe reacted mostly to those elements of poetry that he did not like. According to critic and Poe scholar Edward H. Davidson, Poe studied the poetry of others in order to write better poetry himself. But Davidson also points out, "that instruction he received from other poets' practice marked the startling decline in his own poetic output after 1831; the more Poe thought about poetry, the less he was able to write it."[13]

The poem's popularity made Poe suddenly famous. According to Poe's biographer Arthur H. Quinn, "'The Raven' made an impression probably not surpassed by that of any single piece of American poetry."[14] Its success, however, did not improve his financial situation. He was probably paid either five or ten dollars for it, and vague copyright laws allowed "The Raven" and Poe's other stories and poems to be reprinted worldwide with little if any payment to him.[15]

"The Raven" marked an important point in Poe's writing career; it showed his ability to combine the best of his story-telling techniques with his matured poetic talents.

THE MASTER STORYTELLER

Poe's writing after 1842 showed both his maturity and his mastery of storytelling. Instead of relying solely on supernatural events as the central focus of his stories, he now began to look deeper into his characters, exploring their inner conflicts and psychological makeup. And as Poe's own life experience had increased, his personal struggles began to be reflected in his stories. Such is the case with the story published in the April 1842 issue of *Graham's*, "Life in Death." Later, Poe changed the title of the story to "The Oval Portrait."

Poe's Reflection in "The Oval Portrait"

The narrator of the story takes shelter in a large deserted house and rests in a room with paintings hung on all the walls. His attention is drawn to a painting of a beautiful young woman, and he is amazed by the lifelike expression on the subject's face. He discovers a book in the room which tells about the paintings. Within it he finds the story of the oval-framed portrait. He learns that the woman in the painting was the wife of the artist. The artist loved his art above all, even above his beautiful wife. He convinced her to model for the portrait so that he could preserve her beauty forever. As the picture began to take shape under his brush, he did not realize the effect this had on his wife. The illusion of life that he applied to the canvas drained the life from the living woman. As he put the last touches on the eyes and lips of her image, he discovered that she was dead.

Virginia, Poe, and "The Oval Portrait"

Considering the seriousness of Virginia's illness beginning in January of 1842, it is not surprising that Poe would write a story about the death of a young wife. "The Oval Portrait" is a story about obsession, art, love, and loss. All were subjects Poe knew well. As in so many of his other poems and stories, the death of the beautiful woman is central. The artist in "The Oval Portrait" bears some resemblance in temperament to Poe. He is a "wild and moody man, who became lost in his reveries." He is so focused on the painting that portrays his wife, that he no longer notices the real woman before him. Poe was also devoted to his work for *Graham's Magazine*, which was time-consuming. He usually had a poem, essay or story in each issue, as well as a number of reviews. The January issue had twelve book reviews, and the March issue had nearly twenty.[1] Was Poe projecting his own feelings of guilt for having neglected his young wife as he toiled to make a success of his writing?

Poe scholar Bettina Knapp says that the artist's tragic mistake is in trying to make his wife immortal by freezing her in time, thus denying the natural progression of maturity, old age, and death. By trying to keep his wife the same forever, he loses her forever.[2] Although Poe knew he could not stop the progression of Virginia's disease, it is possible to see "The Oval Portrait" as a projection of that wish to preserve her.

Bloody Terror: "The Masque of the Red Death"

"Life in Death" was followed the next month in *Graham's* by "The Masque of the Red Death." The original inspiration of

"The Masque of the Red Death" tells the story of a man who tries to use his wealth and status to escape death. The gothic tale, whose climactic final scene is illustrated here, has had many different interpretations over the years.

the story may have been a cholera outbreak of 1831 and 1832 which swept first through Asia, then Europe, and eventually through New York, Baltimore, and other areas of the United States. Poe scholar Harry Levin also points out a more direct connection with Poe's life in 1842. Levin comments that, "'the redness and the horror of blood' must have been especially painful for Poe because of an intimate association; we know that disease had first stricken his wife, even while she was singing, with a hemorrhage."[3]

The main character of Poe's story, Prince Prospero, attempts to shut himself off from a plague that is sweeping through his land. He retreats to an abbey, along with a thousand of his friends. He stocks enough provisions to feed and entertain everyone until the danger of the contagious disease is past and welds the gates shuts so that no one can enter or leave. After several months of their confinement, he throws a masquerade ball. At the stroke of midnight, a figure appears whose costume is a death-shroud which appears to be splattered with blood, the sign of the plague. Prospero is furious that someone would come to his party dressed as the Red Death. He chases the shrouded figure from one room to another. When Prospero finally confronts the intruder in the last room and raises a dagger to kill him, Prospero himself falls dead to the floor. Others attempt to grab hold of the intruder, but find that no one is within the shroud. One by one, they all fall dead, conquered by the disease they had tried so hard to shut out.

Levels of Meaning in "The Masque of the Red Death"

Taken literally, this is a story about a proud man who believes his wealth and royal position can give him protection from death. Instead of trying to aid the common people of his kingdom, he selects the lords and ladies to join him in safety. Meanwhile, the rest of his subjects suffer and die outside the welded gates. Prospero's pride leads to his destruction, as he chases the figure, prepared to commit murder in his anger. On this level alone, "The Masque of the Red Death" is a successful horror story, especially as his guests discover that there is no one inside the disguise, and they all die of the same disease.

Interpretations of "The Masque of the Red Death"

As with all of Poe's stories, readers have looked for meaning beyond the literal interpretation. On a symbolic level, most readers see the figure of the Red Death in the story as more than just a fatal disease; it represents death itself. Many critics have discussed the seven rooms with their different colors as representations of Shakespeare's "Seven Ages of Man," from his play *As You Like it*. Prospero's journey through the seven rooms shows his progression through life as he runs toward death. The Prince's many precautions against it are only foolish attempts to avoid death. Like the shrouded figure, Death has no solid form, but is feared above all. This interpretation gives universal meaning to the story, one that applies to all people.

In 1963 literary author Joseph Patrick Roppolo interpreted "The Masque of the Red Death" in a new way. He suggested that, rather than death, the Red Death is actually a symbol of life, "the one 'affliction' shared by all mankind."[4] Roppolo believes that Poe is saying that blood is really "the life force; but even as it suggests life, blood serves as a reminder of death."[5] Roppolo says the costume of the Red Death, having no physical form, is suggestive of man's fear of death. "The intruder," Roppolo says, "is not the plague. Not death itself, but man's creation, his self-aroused and self-developed fear of his own mistaken concept of death."[6] Scott Peeples agrees with Roppolo's interpretation. "Even as he refers to the 'time that flies,'" Peeples tells us, "Poe slows time to a crawl by dwelling on the clock's chimes for a full paragraph, even reminding readers of the number of seconds in an hour, inviting us to reflect—along with Prospero's revelers—on the constant passage of time, each second bringing us closer to death."[7]

Portrait of Insanity: "The Tell-Tale Heart"

Also in 1842, Poe wrote a psychological tale of murder called "The Tell-Tale Heart." Biographer Hervey Allen suggests that this story, with its narrator's concentration on a beating heart, was "probably an imaginative rendering of Poe's attack of heart disease in 1842."[8] Professor Harry Levin suggests that the old man in the story represents John Allan. Levin implies that Poe is expressing his resentment for the years that his foster father tried to control his life. Levin asks, "[I]s this Poe's way of retrospectively dealing with the surveillance of John Allan?"[9]

POE AT THE MOVIES

Perhaps no other writer has had so many movies inspired by his work. IMDb lists over three hundred films credited to Edgar Allan Poe's work. Some are direct interpretations of stories like "The Masque of the Red Death", "The Raven", and "Murders in the Rue Morgue". Others are inspired by Poe himself, such as *The Loves of Edgar Allan Poe*, or even satires such as *The Fall of the Louse of Usher*. A nine-minute silent film called *Edgar Allan Poe* was released in 1909. Over a dozen movie versions of *The Fall of the House of Usher* have been made since 1928.

Poe first submitted the story to *Boston Miscellany*, but the editor there rejected it. Poet James Russell Lowell acquired the story to use in the first issue of his new magazine, the *Pioneer*.[10] In a letter to Lowell in July 1844, Poe listed this story among his own favorites.[11]

The story's narrator is confessing a murder, perhaps to a doctor or lawyer; the identity of his audience is never revealed. The narrator insists that he is not insane. He defends his sanity by giving all the details about the many days and nights he planned to kill the elderly man with whom he lived. The rest of the tale is told in flashback. He had no motive for the killing other than the man's eye: "He had the eye of a vulture—a pale blue eye, with a film over it."[12] As he prepared to kill the man, he heard his victim's heart beating louder in his ear.

After he committed the crime, the narrator cut up the body of the old man and hid it under the floor boards of the house. Later, the police arrived at the house, looking for the old man. The narrator talked cordially with them, while his chair sat on the boards under which the body was hidden. As he sat there, he began to hear the beating of the old man's heart. It grew louder and louder until he could not stand it any longer. The story ends as the narrator jumps up and points at the floor, imploring them to tear up the boards and find the body.

Interpretation and Themes in "The Tell-Tale Heart"

The story is a psychological study of a killer; it is a portrait of insanity. Our narrator says that the old man's "vulture" eye was the reason for the murder, but no rational person could see that as a reason for murder. The opening sentence invites us to question the narrator's sanity. Writer Vincent Buranelli says that Poe does not judge his characters' morality. According to Buranelli, Poe "writes from the standpoint of psychology

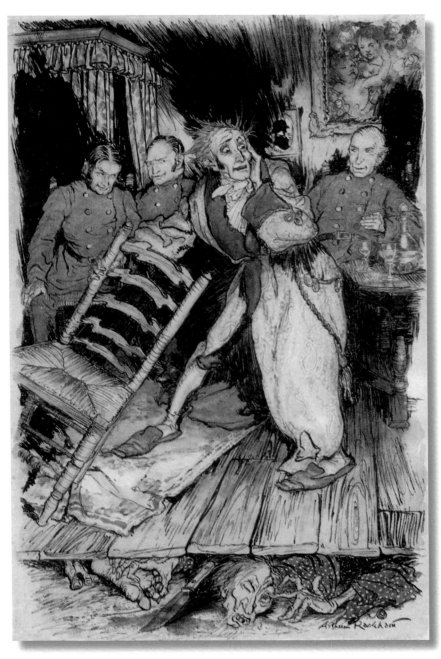

In this scene from "The Tell-Tale Heart," policemen visit the narrator's home in search of the man he has murdered.

rather than ethics. . . . The terrible deeds that abound there result from the pressures of abnormal psychology."[13]

Another theme in the story is the connection between the narrator's emotions and those of his victim. He identifies so much with the old man in his terror, that he says, "I knew what the old man felt, and pitied him."[14] In this paragraph, the narrator describes his own fears and projects them onto the old man. According to Professor E. Arthur Robinson, this leads the narrator to confess his crime. "[S]ince he sees himself in his companion, the result is self-knowledge," says Robinson. "Vision becomes insight, the 'Evil Eye' an evil 'I,' . . . Seeing and seen eye become identical and must be destroyed."[15] In the climax of his identification with his victim, the murderer destroys himself by revealing the crime.

Revenge and Confession: "The Cask of Amontillado"

Poe's story, "The Cask of Amontillado", appeared first in *Godey's Lady's Book* in November 1846. This story is different from Poe's earlier murder stories in several ways. In this case, the motive is clear, the crime has not been discovered, and the killer will not be punished. No reason for the confession is given. The reader may see the narrator's only purpose to boast of the crime, but Scott Peeples suggests that, since the confession comes fifty years after the murder, perhaps this is a deathbed confession given to a priest.[16]

"The Cask of Amontillado" has been praised by critics. Peeples calls this story, "one of Poe's most tightly-constructed tales."[17] Vincent Buranelli describes the story as "finely-wrought, tight, neat, with no loose ends or superfluities," and says, "it strikes with tremendous force within the space of some five pages."[18] Professor David S. Reynolds calls it a "tightly knit tale that reverberates with psychological and moral implications."[19]

In the first sentence we know the victim (Fortunato) and the motive (revenge for an insult). The story begins in a humorous mood, as we see Fortunato dressed in his costume of court jester or fool, in honor of the carnival taking place. We soon learn our narrator's family name is Montresor, because of his association with the family tomb, which he enters with his victim. We also learn that Fortunato's fondness for drink and his pride in his ability to judge wine are the weaknesses that Montresor will use to obtain his revenge. Montresor leads him willingly into the family catacombs with the promise of a taste of Amontillado from the wine cellar. As they walk deeper into the catacombs, the two continue their conversation and the discussion of the Amontillado, as they sample other wine. Along with Fortunato, the reader only learns Montresor's real plan when the two of them, having passed the skeletal remains of many Montresors, come finally to a small crypt. Here, Montresor uncovers mortar and building stones. When he has chained Fortunato to the wall, he uses the trowel he had been carrying under his cloak to seal Fortunato alive within the tomb.

Interpretations and Themes in "The Cask of Amontillado"

The story includes a number of humorous touches and puns that Poe's readers would find amusing, and which contribute to the satire of the story. "The Cask of Amontillado" is sometimes viewed as Poe's own wish for revenge against those who spoke against him. According to Peeples, "Many critics have noted the story's biographical resonance for a writer who believed himself beset by a 'thousand injuries' at the hands of various enemies. . ."[20] By 1846, most readers familiar with Poe were also familiar with his weakness for drink. The drunken Fortunato is dressed like a court jester, a "fool," and his foolishness for drink will lead to his ruin. Professor David S. Reynolds suggests that the story carries a message to warn readers of the danger of drink. Thus, the last wine they sample, De Grave, takes Fortunato one step closer to his death in the grave Montresor constructs for him. The irony of this story coming from Poe's pen would be evident to his readers.[21]

Another pun in the story concerns the secret society, the Masons. According to Reynolds, the organization "was viewed as undemocratic and as a tangible threat to American institutions" during the 1830s.[22] Since "mason" is also a word for a person who lays brick or stone, Fortunato assumes Montresor is joking when he displays a trowel as his sign of membership.

Montresor's feelings about the crime he has committed are not really clear, and a reader's interpretation of the story may be drastically changed by his or her impression of it. A reader who sees the narrator's story of his crime as a boast that he has indeed achieved the perfect revenge he sought, may see this as a story of triumph of pride and vengeance without punishment. But if one accepts Peeple's suggestion that this may be a deathbed confession given to a priest, then we may assume that the crime has haunted Montresor for fifty years. In this case, the final revenge is Fortunato's, since he has rested in peace during the fifty years that Montresor's conscience has tortured him. "If Montresor, for all his cunning, has failed to commit the perfect crime, then the perfect crime cannot be committed—which is precisely Poe's intention," says Peeples.[23]

Montresor prepares to seal Fortunato in the tomb in "The Cask of Amontillado." The idea of being buried alive is present in many of Poe's works.

Poe's Confessing Murderers

The technique of having his tale narrated by the murderer was one of Poe's favorites. He used it in a number of his stories, including "The Black Cat," published the same year as "The Tell-Tale Heart," and also in "The Cask of Amontillado." Although the circumstances of these murders are all different, the narrators' detailed descriptions of the crimes are similar. All the murders are confessed without regret or guilt, and even with a sense of pride in the cleverness shown in the commission of the crimes. Professor Christopher Benfey comments, "Poe's murderers are not so much obsessive killers as obsessive talkers. . . . [T]heir perversity lies not in their need to kill but in their need to tell."[24]

Poe's Masterpiece: "The Raven"

Although Poe had not been writing much poetry in the years prior to 1845, he had been writing a great deal of criticism of the poetry of others, and so defining for himself the characteristics of good verse. He had also been refining his storytelling skills. Now he was ready to combine the two into a narrative poem that would display his mastery of musical poetic techniques.

Plot of "The Raven"

The story of the poem is fairly simple. A young scholar, sitting alone in his room on a stormy winter's night, is studying his books in order to briefly forget his sorrow over the death of his beautiful young lover. He nods off to sleep but is awakened by a peculiar tapping sound. He believes for a moment that the ghost of his lost love has returned to him. He opens the window and a raven flies into the room and perches upon a statue above the door. Amused, the narrator asks the bird's name, and discovers the sole word of the bird's vocabulary: "Nevermore." The narrator then begins to talk to the bird. Not surprisingly, the narrator's every comment is met with the same reply: "Nevermore."

As the narrator's emotions begin to overwhelm him, he first believes the bird is an angel sent by God to comfort his soul, and asks if his love is waiting for him in heaven. Again, the same reply from the bird: "Nevermore." The narrator then becomes hysterical, accusing the bird of being sent by the devil, and orders the bird to leave. Again, the answer is the same: "Nevermore." The poem ends as the narrator, still staring at the raven, resigns himself to the bird's eternal presence and his own eternal grief.

Poetic Devices in "The Raven"

With "The Raven," Poe's careful use of rhyme and meter shows how much he has progressed as a poet. The rhythm consists of a very regular beat that is repeated in each section (stanza) of the poem. Before the end of the second stanza, the reader is accustomed to this beat and expects it. Poe uses an expected beat, but then varies it to make his unexpected use of it stand out. He does this by setting up a regular rhythm, then leaving off the last syllable of some lines to create emphasis. The poem's meter is based on the trochee, a poetic unit consisting of an accented syllable followed by an unaccented one. The first and third lines of each stanza have eight full metric feet of trochees. The second and fourth lines have only seven and a half (that is, they are one syllable short):

/   - / - /   - / - /   - /   - /   - / -
Once upon a midnight dreary, while I pondered, weak and weary,
/ - / -   /   - / - / - / - / - /
Over many a quaint and curious volume of forgotten lore,

/   - / - / - / -   / - / -   /   - / -

While I nodded, nearly napping, suddenly there came a tapping,

/ - /   - / -   / - /   - / -   / -   /

As of some one gently rapping, rapping at my chamber door.

Poe then repeats the shortened rhythm in the fifth line, including a repetition of some words from the end of the previous line:

/   - / - /   - /   -   /   - / -   / -   /

"'Tis some visitor," I muttered, "tapping at my chamber door—

The last line of each stanza has only seven syllables:

/   -   / -   /   -   /

Only this, and nothing more."[25]

Poe employs a repeating rhyme scheme in "The Raven"; The pattern of rhyme at the ends of the lines is identical in all stanzas of the poem. The pattern for each stanza is the same as that shown in stanza five:

Deep into that darkness peering,	
long I stood there wondering, fearing,	A
Doubting, dreaming dreams no mortal	
ever dared to dream before;	B
But the silence was unbroken, and the	
darkness gave no token,	C
And the only word there spoken was the	
whispered word, "Lenore!"	B
This I whispered, and an echo murmured	
back the word, "Lenore!" —	B
Merely this, and nothing more.	B

This marking does not include all the rhyme Poe has used in each stanza, however. We can easily hear the rhyme the poet has used within the lines, called internal rhyme. In each stanza, the word at the middle of the first line rhymes with the word at the end of the line ("peering" and "fearing"). The same is true of the third line of the stanza ("unbroken" and "token"), and an additional rhyme with that at the end of the third line is contained at the middle of the fourth line ("spoken"). Additionally, throughout all eighteen stanzas, the "B" rhymes are all the same, with all rhyming with the refrain of the poem, "Nevermore."

Poe also uses other musical devices of language in "The Raven." Many lines contain alliteration, the repetition of consonant sounds, such as the *n* sound in "While I nodded, nearly napping," and the *d* sound in "Doubting, dreaming dreams no mortal ever dared to dream before." When read aloud, this alliteration causes the reader to slow down and emphasize words, in order to avoid becoming tangled in a tongue-twister. This would contribute to a more dramatic reading, exactly what Poe would want for a poem like this, in which he wished to build suspense.

---

trochee

A foot of poetry consisting of one stressed (accented) syllable, followed by an unstressed syllable.

---

internal rhyme

Poetic technique of rhyming words within one line of poetry.

Narrative Elements of "The Raven"

Poe uses many of the same storytelling elements in "The Raven" that are found in his short stories. As he had done in "The Tell-Tale Heart" and "The Fall of the House of Usher," Poe creates a narrator who is intelligent, but hovering on the brink of madness, so that the reader is never sure if his description of his experience is real or imagined.

As in his short stories, Poe's setting for "The Raven" is important to the story. The setting in "The Raven" contributes to the development of the character of the narrator. The story takes place at midnight in the darkest month of the year, December. Outside the chamber described in "The Raven" a "tempest" (storm) is raging. This disturbance in nature is much like the disturbance of the narrator's state of mind.

Symbolism is also important to this story. In Arabic traditions, the raven is considered a bad omen, a prophet, and a symbol of death. "Aidenn" is the Arabic word for Eden, or paradise. The raven perches on a bust of Pallas, the

> **alliteration**
>
> A poetic technique using repetition of consonant sounds.

goddess of wisdom. The symbolism suggests that our narrator hopes the bird is bringing him knowledge of Lenore from beyond the grave.

Like many of Poe's stories, the plot of "The Raven" begins slowly and calmly. The change in the character's mood happens gradually, with the reader following along as he is first surprised, then amused, then angry at the raven. In many of Poe's stories, even those narrators who have lost their sanity seem at first to be calm and logical. Poe's stories build to a climax of action and emotion. Also, like many of Poe's works, the ending of "The Raven" is ambiguous. The beginning of the poem suggests that the night of the bird's arrival was long ago; how could the raven still be there? The reader does not know whether the bird is actually still sitting there, if he ever was, or if our narrator has only imagined the whole episode.

An engraving of "The Raven" captures the narrator's growing despair as he converses with the bird.

Poe's Identification With His Narrators

Poe was creating fiction so well that it seemed real to his readers. Poe himself soon began to be called "The Raven" as readers associated him with the eccentric characters who narrated his poems and stories. This association even began to apply to Poe's narrators whose actions were influenced by their insanity or their opium use. The stories of Poe's own erratic behavior under the influence of alcohol contributed to his public image. It was an image that Poe's enemies would later use against him.

His Own Worst Enemy

When "The Raven" was published in January 1845, Poe was still working for the *Evening Mirror*. As a literary critic, Poe had a reputation for speaking his mind, no matter whom he offended. Although this had made him enemies in the past, he had peers in the literary community who respected his opinions and his honesty. That respect was severely tested when Poe published a piece in the *Mirror* in which he accused Henry Wadsworth Longfellow, one of the most admired poets of the day, of imitating others. According to Arthur Hobson Quinn, "The result of this 'Longfellow War' was the alienation of such friends as [poet James Russell] Lowell and a growing sense of irritation on the part of fair-minded critics with Poe."[1]

At about the same time, Poe began writing for a new weekly literary publication, *The Broadway Journal*. After contributing several critical essays to the new journal, Poe was offered work as an editor there. In February, he left the *Evening Mirror* to take the position.

Bad Habits, Poor Choices

Despite his new job, things were not going well. Poe's work still was not paying the bills. The *Journal* was not doing well financially, although Poe hoped he could improve that situation. In a letter to F. W. Thomas he complained, "I am as poor now as ever I was in my life—except in hope, which is by no means bankable."[2] According to accounts by some of

Poe's acquaintances, around May of 1845, after over eighteen months of sobriety, he began drinking again.[3] Virginia's health was still poor, and Mrs. Clemm often had to take care of Poe as well. That summer, after Poe was carried home by a friend, Mrs. Clemm expressed her frustrations with him. "Oh! My poor Virginia! She cannot live long! She is wasting away, day by day—for the doctors can do her no good. But if they could, seeing this continually in poor Eddy, would kill her."[4] In June, publishers Wiley and Putnam released a collection of Poe's stories with the title *Tales*. It included twelve of Poe's most well-known stories, including all three of the Dupin stories, as well as others that had already been published many times.

In October, Poe borrowed money to purchase the financially troubled *Journal*. Poe accepted the help of Thomas H. Lane to handle the financial management of the paper, but his drinking had become a serious problem. In December, in the midst of a drinking binge, Poe left the journal at press time without enough material to fill the columns. It was the last straw for Lane, who decided to close up the *Journal*.[5] Lane paid off the debts and the last issue was published on January 3, 1846, with a farewell notice from Poe.[6]

The next spring, Poe returned to the role of critic in *Godey's Lady Book* with a series entitled *The Literati of New York City: Some Honest Opinions at Random Respecting Their Authorial Merits, with Occasional Words of Personality*. It received so much attention that the magazine sold out for that month and *Godey's Lady's Book* produced a second printing of it in the following month to meet the demand.[7]

In May 1846, Poe, Virginia, and Mrs. Clemm moved to Fordham, New York, a few miles outside New York City. Virginia's health was declining rapidly. Poe's health, both physical and mental, was suffering as well. Poe's *Literati* was

Maria Clemm, Poe's aunt, was forced to take care of an ailing Virginia as well as the often intoxicated writer.

gaining notice, but it was not making him popular within the New York literary community. Many of the poets Poe criticized had been featured in Rufus Griswold's book *Poets and Poetry of America*. Poe was brutally honest in his criticism, and some of his comments were not well received. In the first installment, he commented on George H. Colton, editor of the highly regarded literary magazine *The American Review*. Of Colton, Poe said, "I cannot conscientiously call Mr. Colton a good editor, although I think that he will finally be so." Poe described Colton's long poem "Tecumseh" as "insufferably tedious."[8]

Meanwhile, Poe's friendship and correspondence with poet Mrs. Francis Osgood also became a subject of gossip. Rufus Griswold pursued the affections of Mrs. Osgood, who was separated from her husband. Griswold disliked the affectionate tone of the letters between Osgood and Poe, even though their friendship was platonic, and even encouraged by Virginia.[9] It was one more source of bitterness between Poe and Griswold.

Grief and Recovery

As winter approached, Virginia was in the final stages of tuberculosis. A local woman, Mrs. Marie Louise Shew, heard of the family's distress and came to the house to care for Virginia. She provided some medical care and brought other comforts such as warm bedding.[10] Virginia passed away on January 30, 1847, and was buried in a vault that belonged to the landlord of their house. Mrs. Shew stayed at the house to care for Poe, who was dangerously ill himself.[11] He wrote only a few pieces during the remainder of that year. One was a tribute to Mrs. Shew. Another was the poem "Ulalume," a poem about a man approaching the tomb of his lost love.

At the beginning of 1848, Poe finished a piece he considered his masterpiece. He called it a "prose poem," and entitled it *Eureka*. Within its pages he attempted to tie scientific laws together with his theories of poetry and his beliefs about the human mind and soul. He approached G. P. Putnam to publish this new work, and requested the publisher to print fifty thousand copies. Putnam agreed to publish the work that summer, but would only commit to printing five hundred copies.[12] The publisher paid Poe an advance of fourteen dollars.[13]

New Love

After a year of grief, Poe began to develop a new romantic interest. Mrs. Sarah Helen Whitman, a widow from Rhode Island, sent a poem she entitled "To Edgar A. Poe" to a Valentine's Day party attended by many of the literary community in New York. Although neither she nor Poe was present, the poem was read at the party, and word of it reached Poe, whom she addressed in the poem as "The Raven." Helen's poem was later published in a popular magazine, *Home Journal*. Poe responded by sending Helen a copy of his 1831 poem "To Helen." Fanny Osgood wrote to Helen, warning her against becoming involved with Poe, whom she described as "a glorious devil, with large heart and brain."[14] A few months later, Poe wrote a new poem for Mrs. Whitman, which he also entitled "To Helen." The two had not yet met, however, and knew each other only through their letters and their published works.

In July 1848, Poe traveled to Lowell, Massachusetts to deliver a lecture on "Poets and Poetry of America." The lecture was arranged by Mrs. Jane Ermina Locke, and she invited Poe to stay in her home. While staying with Mr. and Mrs. Locke, Poe met Mrs. Nancy Richmond, known to her friends as "Annie." Even though Annie was married, Poe was attracted to her. They began an affectionate friendship and became

Sarah Helen Whitman caught Poe's attention by writing him a poem. Whitman, a Transcendentalist, was a poet as well as an essayist.

quite attached to each other, even though their relationship remained platonic.[15]

That same month, Poe was ready to get back to the business of finding investors for the *Stylus*. He traveled to Richmond to promote the magazine, and while there he spent time with the Mackenzies, the adopted family of his younger sister Rosalie. Accounts by the Mackenzie family and their neighbors suggest that Poe enjoyed this time and appreciated being surrounded by "family." According to biographer Hervey Allen, "For the first time since the death of Virginia, he seems to have cast off gloom, and to have returned to a semblance of the more merry and normal self of boyhood days."[16]

That September, Poe at last made the trip to Providence to meet Sarah Helen Whitman. He immediately began an intense courtship, and by his third day there had proposed marriage to her. She did not give an immediate answer, but promised that she would write him soon with her decision. A few days after Poe's departure, Helen wrote to him and turned down his proposal. She gave several reasons, including her own poor health and her age (she was six years older than Poe). On October 1, 1848, Poe responded with a twelve page letter to her, proclaiming his love for her and answering her objections with his assurance that age did not matter, saying "Has the soul *age*, Helen? Can Immortality regard Time?"[17]

Over the next month, they continued to write, and he asked her to reconsider his proposal of marriage. On November 2, a letter from Helen arrived, but she still did not give him a clear answer. Poe poured out his frustrations to Annie Richmond, who advised him to go to Providence to meet in person with Helen to convince her to marry him. Poe made Annie promise that she would come to him if she heard that he was dying.[18]

Rejection

Upon arriving in Providence, Poe's despair was more than he could bear. He was both sick with his love for the married Annie and convinced that Helen would again reject him. Instead of going to visit Helen, Poe boarded a train to Boston. Once there, he purchased two ounces of laudanum, a mixture of opium and alcohol which was commonly available as a medicine. He intended to take his own life with the drug. He wrote a letter to Annie telling her where she could find him in Boston, and reminding her of her promise to come to him on his deathbed. He took half of the drug and went to mail the letter. Before he could make it to the post office, the drug overcame him, and he became violently ill. He was helped by a friend, but remained ill from the effects of the drug for several days.

On November 7, Poe returned to Providence to see Helen. Over the next few days they met several times. She showed him some of the letters she had received from people who warned her against marrying him. Before he left Providence on November 13, however, she agreed to marry him, on the condition that he must quit drinking.

By mid-December, plans were proceeding for the wedding. On December 20, Poe lectured on the "Poetic Principle" in Providence to a large crowd, and the couple made their plans to be married in just a few days. On the evening of the twenty-second, however, Poe arrived at a social gathering at Helen's house, and had been drinking. He promised her, in the presence of her friends that he would not drink again, but an acquaintance told her that Poe ordered a glass of wine at the bar of his hotel the following morning. She ended the engagement immediately, and Poe left Providence on the train that evening to return home to New York.[19]

Poe turned to Annie Richmond for comfort. As he recovered from his failed relationship with Helen during the next six months, Poe continued to express his affection for Annie, despite the fact that she was married. Biographer Quinn describes Poe's conflicted feelings for these two women as "evidence of the duality of Poe's nature," and says that Poe "loved 'Annie' as a man loves a woman, while he loved Helen Whitman as a poet loves a poetess."[20] Jeffrey Meyers suggests that perhaps Poe drank purposely to break the engagement to Helen "because he felt he loved the unattainable Annie more than the available Helen."[21]

In the winter of 1848-49 Poe was ready to return to his writing. In a letter to Annie that January, he told her, "I am so busy now, and feel so full of energy. Engagements to write are pouring in upon me every day."[22] He also reported that he had sent the poem *Landor's Cottage* to one magazine and an article on literary criticism to another. He had also sent fifty pages of literary comments to be published in the *Southern Literary Messenger* over the next several months.[23] In March, he sent a poem entitled "To Annie" to her. Despite his struggles, some of Poe's best writing was still to come.

The Last Poems

P oe struggled both personally and professionally throughout his life, but the two years following Virginia's death
were even more difficult as he dealt with his own drinking
problem and his troubled relationships. When he regained his
energy to write in late 1848, he returned to his poetry with a
maturity and mastery that allowed him to produce some of his
best works.

The Music of "The Bells"

The earliest known version of this poem did not even reveal
Poe as its author. According to a story told by Mrs. Marie
Louise Shew, who had cared for Virginia during her final days,
Poe came to her house in early May 1848, upset and convinced
that he could not write another poem. She said that when the
bells from a nearby church began to ring, she wrote "The Bells
by E. A. Poe" on a sheet of paper and placed it before him.
Then he began to write the poem.[1]

The original version of the poem was only two stanzas
long, and was credited "by Mrs. M. L. Shew." A few months
later, Poe revised the poem slightly and added the occasions of
the wedding and the funeral.

But the biggest change came with the third version, probably written around December 1848. The third version was
expanded to one hundred and twelve lines, and creates four
distinct moods. Poe scholar and critic Burton R. Pollin, has

For every sound that floats
From out their ghostly throats
    Is a groan.
And the people — ah, the people
Who live up in the steeple

        All alone,
And who, tolling, tolling, tolling,
    In that muffled monotone,
Feel a glory in so rolling
    On the human heart a stone —
They are neither man nor woman —
They are neither brute nor human,
But are pestilential carcases disparted from their souls —
        Called Ghouls : —
    And their king it is who tolls : —
And he rolls, rolls, rolls, rolls
    A Pæan from the bells !
    And his merry bosom swells
        With the Pæan of the bells !
    And he dances and he yells ;
Keeping time, time, time,
In a sort of Runic rhyme,
        To the Pæan of the bells —
        Of the bells : —

The last stanza of "The Bells," handwritten by Poe.

called the original version "indeed a poor thing," but says the later version "had been profoundly altered into a major work, not far behind The Raven [for his] extraordinary use of repetition for musical and rhetorical effects."[2]

The longer version of the poem has four numbered stanzas. The first part describes the silver sleigh bells that jingle merrily under a night sky full of stars. The second stanza is about golden wedding bells that foretell happiness for the married couple. The third section describes the clanging of alarm bells that ring on the firehouse and tell of danger and fright. In the final stanza iron bells ring a death knell for funeral mourners. At first the sound is sad, but then it changes to a wild dance tune for the ghouls that celebrate death.

Poetic Devices in "The Bells"

The poem's structure is interesting because, unlike "The Raven", the stanzas are not alike. The first stanza is the shortest, only fourteen lines. The second stanza has twenty-one lines, and the third is even longer with thirty four. The final stanza has forty-four lines. There are many similarities in all the stanzas, including the chorus in the last three lines of each stanza which is similar, but not identical, to the first: "From the bells, bells, bells, bells,/ Bells, bells, bells—/ From the jingling and the tinkling of the bells."[3]

Like "The Raven," this poem contains many musical qualities. It has both steady and repeating end rhyme, as well as internal rhyme in many of the lines, such as "To the swinging and the ringing" and "To the rhyming and the chiming." It contains a great deal of repetition of consonant sounds, or alliteration, as in "What a tale of terror, now, their turbulency tells!" Poe also uses repeated vowel sounds, called assonance, in lines such as the long *o* sound in "From the molten-golden notes."

The most notable sound device is onomatopoeia, the use of words that imitate the sounds they name. Words that describe the sounds of the bells like "tinkle," "clang," and "tolling" create different sounds for the bells when spoken. This device creates the moods of the different types of bells and makes the poem very effective when read aloud. Biographer and literary critic Arthur Hobson Quinn says, "'The Bells' is one of the most successful verbal imitations of sound in the English language."[4]

In addition, the sounds of the words in each section carry the mood of the subject of that section. The repetition of the short vowel sounds in the first section, in words like "twinkle," "jingling," even "tintinnabulation," allow the words to be spoken lightly and quickly to add to the mood of "merriment" of the sleigh bells in that stanza. The repetition of the *l* sounds in the second section in words like "mellow," "golden," and "dwells" gives a more flowing sound to this stanza. This slows the poem down and makes it more smooth and suggestive of the mature love of the married couple. The third part, with its sharp alliteration in the *t* sounds of "What a tale their terror tells," and the onomatopoetic sounds of "clanging," "jangling," and "shriek," make stronger sounds that suggest the fear caused by the alarm bells. Finally, the long *o* sounds of the final section create the same type of mournful sound

---

assonance

A poetic technique using repetition of vowel sounds.

---

onomatopoeia

Poetic technique of using words which, when spoken, make a sound like they describe (Examples: "pop," "hiss").

---

that Poe had already made famous in "The Raven." The sound "rolls," "floats," and "tolls" in a "monotone." Vincent Buranelli comments, "Here, where the appeal to the ear is immediate and inescapable, Poe achieves one of his most remarkable successes. World literature can scarcely show a more triumphant handling of onomatopoeia—suggestiveness and meaning conveyed though the medium of sounds."[5]

The Unattainable Dream of "Eldorado"

At about the same time as he was revising "The Bells," Poe wrote to a friend about the "gold-fever" sweeping the nation with the discovery of gold in the West. It was probably also about this time that he wrote the poem, "Eldorado."[6] According to Vincent Buranelli, Eldorado was a common name for the dream of the mythical gold field that would make a person rich. It also applied to any dream of some imagined place where one's wishes are fulfilled. Poe used the word both ways in this poem of only twenty-four lines. Unlike "The Bells," the poem has a structure that remains the same through all four stanzas. Each stanza is six lines long, and each has the same rhyme scheme and meter.

The first stanza tells of a knight who rides forth "singing a song" in search of Eldorado. In the second stanza the knight has grown old and becomes discouraged because he still has not found his dream. In the third stanza, he is ready to die when he meets a spirit and asks him where he can find Eldorado. The spirit tells him his dream is "Over the Mountains of the Moon, Down the Valley of the Shadow."

Poetic Techniques and Meaning in "Eldorado"

The poem's brevity and its lack of relation to Poe's usual themes of love and fear of death have caused it to be ignored by most

Poe critics. Also, the regularity of the rhyme and meter has caused some to consider it little more than a quaint, sing-song "jingle." Although critic Buranelli admits that "Eldorado," like "The Bells," is light verse, both poems have meaningful messages. "Both are jingles," he says, "but jingles with depth."[7] In "Eldorado," Poe seems to be suggesting that our ultimate dreams are as unreachable as the moon. They may only be found after we have passed through the "Valley of the Shadow," a suggestion of death, as referred to in Psalm 23 in the Bible. Scott Peeples suggests that Poe may be expressing his own disappointment with his life and his own quest to create a higher form of art through his poetry. According to Peeples, "His life consisted largely of personal tragedies, professional frustrations, and unrelenting poverty, throughout which he

Poe was living in this cottage in New York when he wrote "Annabel Lee," his last complete poem.

pursued a higher realm of consciousness through art and speculated on art's connections with the eternal."[8]

The Tender "Annabel Lee"

In a letter to Annie Richmond in May 1849, Poe told her of a new poem he had finished.[9] This poem, "Annabel Lee" was probably the last poem Poe wrote. Poe, believing that his rival Rufus Griswold was now his friend, asked Griswold to be his literary executor, in charge of publishing collections of Poe's work after his death. He sent "Annabel Lee" to Griswold in May of that year.[10]

Both Sarah Helen Whitman and the poet Sarah Anna Lewis claimed to be the Annabel Lee of the poem. Elmira Shelton, Poe's sweetheart from his teenage years, claimed that she was "Annabel Lee." In a letter to Rufus Griswold in 1850, Mrs. Francis Osgood claimed that Poe's wife Virginia was the young bride who died in the poem. Most critics today accept Mrs. Osgood's claim, although critic T. O. Mabbott and others are quick to remind readers that this poem, like Poe's other works, is more fiction than autobiography.[11] Osgood described "Annabel Lee" as "by far the most natural, simple, tender and touchingly beautiful of all his songs."[12]

"Annabel Lee" tells of the love of a young couple in a "kingdom by the sea." Their love was so deep that even the angels envied them and sent a cold wind that made Annabel Lee so sick that she died. The narrator mourns his lost love, but also says that their love is so strong that it lives on in his dreams and in their souls which will forever be joined.

Poetic Techniques in "Annabel Lee"

Like the other poems of this last period of Poe's life, this poem is musical and creates a mood to match the subject of the poem.

TWENTIETH CENTURY POE

Vincent Price (1911-1993) was an American actor who starred in eight different film adaptations of Edgar Allan Poe stories, many of them directed by Roger Corman. In addition to his chilling roles in movies like *The Tomb of Ligea, Tales of Terror*, and *The Fall of the House of Usher*, Price also starred in *An Evening of Edgar Allan Poe*, a one-hour film in which he reads several Poe stories. Price also starred in many movies in both dramatic and comedic roles, but he was best known for his horror films. In addition to his movie roles, he recorded several albums on which he read Poe stories. Because of his many roles in Poe movies, he became almost a representation of Poe himself for audiences.

Vincent Price

Bettina Knapp says the poem "should be read aloud to be fully appreciated, for its tones and timbres, meter and metrics, for the flow of the feelings involved."[13] With its alternating lines of four beats and three beats, the poem flows smoothly and regularly, almost like the waves on the beach of the "kingdom by the sea." Every other line throughout the first four stanzas of the poem rhymes with the long *e* sound of "sea," and follow the same pattern as the first stanza.

> It was many and many a year ago,
> In a kingdom by the sea,
> That a maiden there lived whom you may know
> By the name of Annabel Lee;
> And this maiden she lived with no other thought
> Than to love and be loved by me.[14]

This pattern continues until stanza five, which has an odd number of lines—seven, and the second and third line rhyme with each other and have only three beats each. Stanza six ends with two rhyming couplets in a row, and also varies the meter because lines five and six each have four beats, and lines seven and eight both have only three. The variation prevents the poem from becoming monotonous, with too much repetition of the pattern of the first four stanzas. This variation also emphasizes the meaning over the music of the verse in the final four lines, the lines that describe the continuation of their love for eternity.

Despite the tragedies and disappointments of Poe's life, his poetic powers were still strong in 1849. These last poems, usually considered among Poe's best, were not well known during Poe's lifetime, but would become widely printed and quoted after their famous author's death.

Poe's Final Days

By the spring of 1849, Poe had spent nine years with the dream of publishing his own literary magazine, only to be disappointed when the financial backing for it fell through. But in April of that year, he was contacted by Edward Patterson, a young newspaperman and print shop owner from Illinois. He offered to publish Poe's *Stylus*, and to make Poe editor and half-owner of the magazine. In order to get it started, they would need to find one thousand subscribers.[1]

Lost and Found

Poe left New York on June 29, for a lecture tour to raise money and generate interest in the *Stylus*. His first stop was to be Richmond, Virginia, but instead of going straight to Richmond, he apparently stopped off in Philadelphia. Soon after arriving in Philadelphia, Poe discovered that his suitcase with his written speeches was missing. On about July 1, Poe began drinking and was put into jail for a short time. While there, he suffered from hallucinations caused by withdrawal from alcohol, a condition known as *delirium tremens*. During the next week, several acquaintances reported seeing him at different times, but no one knows just what he did.

On the tenth, Poe returned to the train station to look for his missing suitcase. The suitcase had been found, but both of his speeches were missing from it. On the twelfth, several friends of Poe's each contributed some money to purchase him a train ticket and they escorted him to the train depot. On July 14, Poe at last arrived in Richmond, but he could not give a clear account of where he had been or what he had done. He wrote to Maria Clemm about his experiences in Philadelphia and his decision that those experiences should "prove a warning to me for the rest of my days."[2]

Poe's visit in Richmond included both business and social meetings. He spent some time with his sister Rosalie at the Mackenzie home. He also visited with the editor of the *Southern Literary Messenger*, and made plans to deliver some lectures on the Poetic Principle. On August 17, Poe delivered his lecture before a large and enthusiastic crowd at the Exchange Hotel. A local newspaper commented, "All present must have highly appreciated the entertainment, and we trust that Mr. Poe will give us another illustration of his fine literary acquirements."[3]

Romance Rekindled

The trip to Richmond also offered a romantic opportunity for Poe. Elmira Royster Shelton, Poe's sweetheart from his teenage years, was now a widow, still living in Richmond. Poe visited her, and they rekindled their romance. Elmira's family objected to the relationship. They knew the widow would give up a large portion of her inheritance from her husband if she remarried, according to the conditions of his will. Secondly, Poe's reputation for his difficulties with drink and women troubled them. Despite their objections, Elmira and Poe began making plans for their wedding.

A letter from Edward Patterson to Poe on August 21 outlined Patterson's firm commitment to begin publishing the *Stylus* beginning with the July 1850 issue, if Poe could sign up the needed subscribers.[4] To demonstrate his commitment to changing his habits, Poe joined the Richmond chapter of the Sons of Temperance on August 27. In doing so, he made a public and formal agreement to give up drinking forever. Within a few days, he had purchased a wedding ring.[5] He made plans to return to his home in New York in order to bring Mrs. Clemm and their belongings to Richmond, where they would live with Elmira after the wedding.

On September 25, he and Rosalie visited the home of Susan Talley and her family, near the Mackenzie's home. Later, Susan would say that Poe seemed to be looking forward to his future. "He declared that the last few weeks in the society of his old and new friends had been the happiest that he had known for many years, and that when he again left New York he should there leave behind all the trouble and vexation of his past life."[6]

The Tragic End

On September 26, Poe visited Elmira once more before he left Richmond. Later, some friends walked with him to the dock to board the boat bound for Baltimore. From Baltimore, he planned to take a train for the rest of his journey. According to those friends, Poe was sober at the time he boarded the boat. The steamship left Richmond at 4 a.m. on September 27, and arrived in Baltimore in the early morning of September 28.[7]

Five days later, Poe was found, lying semi-conscious, outside a tavern in Baltimore. He appeared to be drunk. His friend, Dr. Joseph Snodgrass, heard that he was in distress. Poe was admitted to a hospital. For the next four days, he went in and out of consciousness, but was never coherent enough to tell what had happened to him after he left Richmond. On October 7, he died. No autopsy was performed to determine the exact cause of death. His cousin, Neilson Poe, was called, and Poe was buried in the family plot in the Presbyterian Cemetery in Baltimore on October 8.

This image of Poe was made shortly before his death. The circumstances surrounding the end of Poe's life remain a mystery to this day.

Poe's death did not end the questions and gossip about his life. If anything, the mysterious circumstances of his death intensified the talk. No one knew just what Poe had done from the time his ship arrived in Baltimore on September 28 until he was found on October 3. Early reports indicated that Poe had died as a result of a drunken spree, and *The New York Herald* reported that he had died of *delirium tremens*.

Mystery Unsolved

Those who have examined the many strange circumstances of Poe's death have suggested several different possible solutions. Mrs. Elizabeth Oakes Smith, a poet who met Poe several years before his death, published an article in 1867 in which she stated that Poe died at the hand of someone who was avenging "a woman, who considered herself injured by him."[8]

In 1873 John R. Thompson, editor of the *Southern Literary Messenger,* presented a new theory regarding Poe's death. Poe was discovered on October 3, an election day, outside a tavern that was used as a polling place in Baltimore. In those days, political corruption in Baltimore included a practice known as "cooping." Men employed by supporters of a candidate seized poor or drunken men on the street and held them for a few days under guard, during which time the men were robbed and given drinks or drugs. On Election Day, these men were then led from one polling place to another to vote repeatedly for the candidate. When the polls closed or the men were unable to vote anymore, they were often abandoned on the sidewalk or in an alley.

Poe was often described by those who knew him as being very particular about his appearance. When he was carried to the hospital in Baltimore, he was wearing ill-fitting and ragged clothing, very unlike any he would have chosen to wear.

Thompson suggested that Poe had been "cooped" in Baltimore, robbed of his clothing, and left on the sidewalk outside the polling place. Thompson delivered a series of lectures in 1873 in which he repeated this story.[9] Later, Thompson's theory was picked up by Poe's biographers, including John Ingram, and presented in their books.[10]

In his 1941 biography of Poe, Arthur Hobson Quinn offered a theory to account for Poe's whereabouts between September 28 when he left Richmond and October 3 when he was found in Baltimore. He suggested that Poe left Baltimore and traveled to Philadelphia, where he was expected to meet with Mrs. Marguerite St. Leon Loud. Mrs. Loud's husband had offered to pay Poe one hundred dollars to edit a volume of his wife's poetry.[11] Quinn cites a statement by one of Poe's friends who claimed that Poe came to Philadelphia, stayed two or three days, become ill, and later left for the train station, telling his friends that he was going to New York. They believed that he had simply caught the wrong train and gone back to Baltimore instead. Quinn also discusses the "cooping" theory, although he says there is no real evidence to support it.[12]

In 1998 author John Evangelist Walsh examined the many pieces of evidence and personal statements and approached the mystery in a manner similar to that of Poe's famous detective, Dupin. Walsh refers to Elizabeth Oakes Smith's statement that Poe had been beaten as revenge for some insult against a woman, and ties that testimony to the fact that Elmira Shelton's family was against her engagement to Poe. Walsh then refers to a statement from a train conductor who claimed Poe had been followed by two men on a train from Baltimore to Philadelphia. He concludes that Elmira's two brothers followed Poe from Baltimore to Philadelphia, intending to intimidate Poe into breaking the engagement. He suggests that Poe bought the shabby clothing at a second-hand store in Philadelphia in order to disguise himself, then caught a train back to Baltimore to lose his pursuers. Walsh believes the brothers caught up with Poe again when he returned to Baltimore. There they forced him to drink, and left him in a public place where he would be recognized, knowing that news of his drunkenness would get back to Elmira and she would cancel the engagement.[13]

While Walsh does a convincing job of creating a story which ties together many separate pieces of information, much of his story is based on guesses.

In addition to all of the theories that suggest foul play, others have proposed a variety of medical reasons for Poe's death. Biographer Jeffrey Meyers believed the author's cause of death was a diabetic coma. He points to the symptoms Poe was said to be suffering at the end of his life: hallucinations, tremors, anxiety, and sweating.[14] A researcher in Maryland concluded the author died of rabies based on these same symptoms.[15] Still another researcher tested some of his hairs and found a high level of mercury, suggesting that may have poisoned him.[16]

Finally, another possible medical explanation is that Poe may have suffered from a brain tumor. When his body was exhumed twenty-six years after his death, it was badly decomposed, but one worker reported that there was a solid mass inside Poe's skull. Although Poe's brain would have decayed long before, a forensic pathologist has said that brain tumors can calcify after death and turn into hard lumps.[17] Is it possible Poe suffered from a brain tumor? Like several of the other theories, it might explain some of his symptoms and behavior in the days and months before his death.

More than one hundred fifty years later, the circumstances of the events leading to Poe's death remain a mystery.

According to the account told by Dr. J. J. Moran, who cared for Poe during the last few days of his life, Poe sometimes regained enough consciousness to speak clearly, but could never tell what had happened to him. His last words were "Lord help my poor soul."[18]

Griswold's Revenge

On October 9, an obituary appeared in the *New York Tribune.* "Edgar Allan Poe is dead. He died in Baltimore the day before yesterday. This announcement will startle many, but few will be grieved by it." It went on to claim that Poe "had few or no friends." Although the author praised Poe's stories and poems, he added that "as a critic, he was more remarkable as a dissector of sentences than as a commenter upon ideas."[19] The obituary's author, "Ludwig," was later proven to be Poe's old rival, Rufus W. Griswold.

Griswold published a collection of Poe's works in 1850. In it, he included a "Memoir of the Author" in which he claimed that Poe was a drug addict. Because several of Poe's stories had narrators who claimed to be opium users, many people believed Griswold's claims. Biographer Arthur Hobson Quinn points to Poe's suicide attempt of 1848 as evidence that he was not an opium addict as some writers have said. Quinn makes the point that if Poe were regularly using opium, he would not have had such a strong reaction to the laudanum he took.[20]

Griswold published many of Poe's letters, but altered some of them in order to give the worst possible impression of Poe. Unfortunately, Griswold's writings were accepted for many years as truth, and other biographers used them as sources of information about Poe.

Certainly, some of Poe's problems were caused by his drinking. Arthur Hobson Quinn suggests that perhaps Poe's

Rufus W. Griswold, whose writings Poe had criticized, did his best to tarnish the author's memory after his death.

drinking was not a personality flaw or a lack of willpower, but a physical weakness over which he had little control. Poe's father, David Poe, was noted in a theater program of 1809 as being absent from a performance because of "indisposition." According to Quinn, "'Indisposition' is a term used often in theatrical notices of that day to cover intoxication, which would support the theory that accounts by heredity for Edgar Poe's infirmity."[21] Quinn also refers to a letter from Poe's friend Frederick Thomas, in which Thomas insists that Poe had a very low tolerance for alcohol. According to Thomas, "[I]f he took but one glass of weak wine or beer or cider, the Rubicon of the cup was passed with him, and it almost always ended in excess and sickness."[22] While this possible physical cause of Poe's drinking problems may help readers today understand this side of Poe, it does not change the negative effects that Poe's drinking had on his reputation in his own time. It only made it easier for Griswold to further damage Poe's image.

According to Professor I. M. Walker, "Griswold's 'Memoir,' coming as it did from Poe's authorized editor, was generally regarded as an authentic account of a willfully ruined life.... [I]t was Griswold's caricature—part fiend and degenerate, part wasted genius—that prevailed in the English-speaking world for two decades and more."[23]

Despite Griswold's attempts at character assassination, however, Poe is still regarded by many as an artist and genius. His work has retained the respect of scholars and critics from Poe's time to ours.

Evermore: Poe's Legacy

Poe was both admired and hated in his own time. Although many people appreciated his writing, he angered many writers with his criticism. James Russell Lowell, in his 1848 poem "A Fable for Critics," described Poe as, "Three-fifths of him genius and two-fifths sheer fudge."[1] Others, however, were more admiring of the man known as "The Raven." Shortly after Poe's death, George Washington Peck wrote, "That Poe will long be considered, as he is now, a poet of singular genius, there can be no question."[2]

Differing Critical Opinions

In 1909, author George Bernard Shaw said, "Poe constantly produced magic where his greatest contemporaries produced only beauty. . . . "The Raven," "The Bells," and "Annabel Lee" are as fascinating at the thousandth repetition as at the first."[3]

Poe's *Poetic Principle*, probably written within the last year of his life, summarized his theories of the elements of good poetry. Literary critic Edward Zuk has argued that Poe's ideas changed the popular styles of poetry for many years after his death. In fact, Zuk calls it "[o]ne of the most influential—and therefore one of the most dangerous—essays in American literature," because its ideas were so restrictive that some poets could not express themselves within Poe's guidelines.

Charles Baudelaire, a famous French poet, spent years translating Poe's works into French.

"'The Poetic Principle' foresees and justifies that narrowing of poetic range which took hold of the twentieth century, that conception of poetry which encouraged poets to limit themselves to a few well-used lyric types striving for intense, emotional effects."[4]

French writers and poets admired Poe much more than the British or even American writers of the day. They praised his originality and experimentation with new forms of poetry, as well as the musical quality of his verse. But American critics through the years have seemed skeptical of the praise of the French for Poe's work. Novelist Aldous Huxley guessed that perhaps Baudelaire and Poe's other French admirers simply did not understand English well enough to realize Poe's faults as a poet. In a letter to French poet Paul Valéry, Huxley stated, "It is only among foreigners, endowed in this case with a fortunate deafness and blindness, that Poe can enjoy a reputation as a great poet." Huxley said that almost all of Poe's poetry displayed "a vulgarity in the choice of words, in the verbal harmony and especially in the rhythms, a great many of which have for us almost the quality of the popular waltz or the polka."[5] Despite this controversy, Poe and his work continue to fascinate readers in the twenty-first century.

Poe's Legacy in Literature

Considering the relatively short life and career of Poe, his lasting impact is impressive. The wide variety of writing, including literary criticism, poetry, detective stories, horror, psychological thrillers, fantasy, and more, has broadened Poe's influence into all these areas. Despite the differing views of critics through the years, there is no disputing the fact that Edgar Allan Poe's work influenced many writers of his own time as well as those who followed.

Literary Criticism and Theories

Although Poe's criticisms angered many of the writers of his day, he is often considered to be the first great literary critic in America. In his work for *Burton's, Graham's,* and other magazines, he wrote dozen of reviews of other writers' works. In his time, most literary reviewers practiced what Poe called "puffery." That is, they praised the work of other authors in order to promote sales and, in some cases, to invite positive reviews of their own work in turn.[6] Poe would have none of this. He was determined to hold true to his standards for literature. George Graham once said, "Literature to him was religion; and he, its high-priest."[7]

Unlike other critics of his time, Poe not only offered honest criticism, but also presented his original theories of fiction and poetry. His definitions of good fiction and the ideas he presented in his *Poetic Principle* are often used in writing courses today to help writers strive for qualities like unity of effect and beauty for its own sake.

Poe's Poetic Legacy

Although he is often remembered most for his fiction, Poe's first writing, and his first love, was his poetry. In contrast to many poets of his day who believed poetry had to convey a moral lesson, Poe sought to explore the beauty of language and ideas in his poetry. Much of his verse employs musical qualities best enjoyed when the poem is read aloud.

The French Symbolists Paul Valéry and Charles Baudelaire were fascinated by Poe's work. Baudelaire once declared, "Every morning I will pray to God, the reservoir of all strength and justice, to my father, to Mariette and to Poe, as intercessors."[8] Professor Jeffrey Meyers points out that many of Baudelaire's works incorporated ideas, images, and even language from Poe's works. Elements of Poe's poem "To Helen" and images and language from the stories "The Black Cat," "The Fall of the House of Usher," "The Man of the Crowd," and others are present in the work of Baudelaire.[9]

Despite the critics who belittle Poe's poetic works, they are still popular today. No anthology of American literature would be complete without "The Raven," "Eldorado," "The Bells," and "Annabel Lee." Besides their appeal to readers of all ages, Poe's poems are useful as illustrations of poetic techniques to help readers better understand the fundamentals of poetry.

Detective Stories and Mysteries

Poe is often described as "the father of the modern detective story." In "The Murders in the Rue Morgue," Poe established the formula for the detective story that became his signature. Poe introduced his detective, C. Auguste Dupin, as a master of analytical thought and observation. He gave him a crime that seemed impossible to solve, and one that had baffled police. He also gave him a companion who could not follow the clues as well, thus requiring Dupin to explain his methods. At the end of the story, the detective reveals all the clues within the story and tells how they led to the solution.

When Sir Arthur Conan Doyle introduced his character, Sherlock Holmes, in 1887, the resemblance was immediately apparent. Doyle never denied that Poe was his inspiration; in fact, Doyle's stories sometimes included elements so similar to Poe's that he was accused of plagiarism. When Doyle visited the United States on a lecture tour in 1894, he told the audience that Poe's Dupin was "the best detective in fiction." He continued, "Dupin is unrivaled. It was Poe who taught the possibility of making a detective story a work of literature."[10]

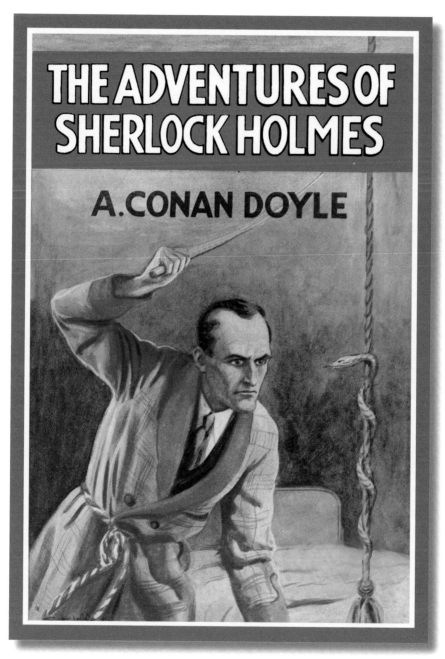

A copy of *The Adventures of Sherlock Holmes* by Sir Arthur Conan Doyle. The author expressed his admiration for Poe's detective Dupin, who was likely a model for Holmes.

Dozens of versions of both Poe's and Doyle's stories have been produced for stage, radio theater, movies, and television.

Poe's formula for the detective story became the standard for many authors of mysteries. Agatha Christie's stories featuring Hercule Poirot (introduced in 1920) and Miss Marple (introduced in 1927) follow a similar pattern. Other detectives like Philo Cance and Ellery Queen were popular around the same time. Younger readers have enjoyed teen detectives like the Hardy Boys and Nancy Drew since 1927 and 1930, respectively.

When television broadcast began, detective shows became a staple of home entertainment. Each decade has brought new characters to the small screen: Perry Mason in the fifties, Columbo in the seventies, and Jessica Fletcher (*Murder, She Wrote)* in the eighties. More recent detective characters include Father Dowling, Monk, and Castle, to name just a few.

So great is the legacy of Poe in detective fiction that Doyle once remarked, "It is the irony of Fate that he should have died in poverty, for if every man who wrote a story which was indirectly inspired by Poe were to pay a tithe toward a monument it would be such as would dwarf the pyramids."[11]

In recognition of Poe's contribution to the genre, each year The Mystery Writers of America award writers in several categories of mysteries with "The Edgars." The award recognizes the year's best work in the field, and includes a statuette of Poe.

Psychological Horror and Science Fiction

Poe's dark tales of death, madness, and terror, sometimes referred to as his Gothic tales, have also influenced writers, film makers, and others. Gothic stories of ghosts and drafty castles were around before Poe's time, and he used these settings and ideas in some of his stories. But Poe went deeper than the dark corners of castles for his horror: He explored the darkest corners of the human mind.

Filmmaker Alfred Hitchcock is known for such suspenseful thrillers as *Psycho, Vertigo,* and *The Birds.* He discovered the work of Poe when he was sixteen. It helped him understand why people like stories that scare them.

> I went straight to my room, took the cheap edition of his *Tales of the Grotesque and Arabesque,* and began to read. I still remember my feelings when I finished "The Murders in the Rue Morgue." I was afraid, but this fear made me discover something I've never forgotten since: fear, you see, is an emotion people like to feel when they know they're safe.[12]

Dennis R. Perry, a professor at the University of Missouri, draws direct comparisons between themes in several of Hitchcock's movies and in Poe's stories. According to Perry, Hitchcock acknowledged his debt to Poe when he said, "Very likely it's because I was so taken with the Poe stories that I later made suspense films."[13]

Novelist Stephen King has also credited Poe as an inspiration in his horror novels. King's stories often include characters whose mental illness leads them to violence. In a lecture in 2010, he told an audience, "Poe was the first writer to write about main characters who were bad guys or who were mad guys, and those are some of my favorite stories."[14] King even patterned a story after Poe's "The Tell-Tale Heart." He entitled it "The Old Dude's Ticker," and used many of the same elements present in Poe's story.

Poe was also a pioneer in the genre of science fiction. His 1835 story "Hans Phaall, A Tale," concerns a trip to the moon in a hot air balloon. In 1939, Poe's story "The Man That Was Used Up" appeared in *Burton's.* The narrator of that story tells of a man who was nearly killed but was reconstructed of manufactured parts. Author Jules Verne discovered the works of Poe when he was a boy and considered him his favorite author.[15] Verne later became the first author to specialize in futuristic science-based fiction. His novels include *Journey to the Center of the Earth* and *Around the World in Eighty Days.* In 1864 he wrote *Edgar Allan Poe and his Works.* In 1897 Verne published *An Antarctic Mystery*, a two-volume story that continues the tale of Poe's *Narrative of Arthur Gordon Pym.* Today, Verne's story would be considered "fan fiction."

Horror and science fiction writer Ray Bradbury was also inspired by Poe's work. Like Hitchcock and Verne, he read Poe's stories when he was young, and it shaped his own writing. "I wrote at least a thousand words a day from the age of twelve on. For years, Poe was looking over one shoulder, while Wells, Burroughs, and just about every other writer in *Astounding* and *Weird Tales* looked over the other."[16] In tribute to Poe, Bradbury placed specific references to "The Fall of the House of Usher" and "The Cask of Amontillado" in his story *Usher II,* in which a millionaire builds a theme park on Mars patterned after the House of Usher.[17]

Continuing Influence of Poe

In the years since his death, Poe's popularity has continued to grow. Nearly every American recognizes "The Raven," whether recited in its original form or in a television commercial parody. Dozens of movies have been made of Poe's stories, including many versions of "The Tell-Tale Heart," "The Fall of the House of Usher," and "The Masque of the Red Death." According to the E. A. Poe Society, "First printings of Poe's books sell for thousands, his manuscripts for tens of thousands. His 1827 *Tamerlane and Minor Poems* is one of the most valuable books ever printed in the United States. Ironically, in death Poe has magnificently achieved what evaded him during his lifetime—commercial success."[18]

It seems like Poe's fans just can't get enough of him. Even social media includes Poe fans and tributes. Poe has at least two Facebook pages. One is listed as "Edgar Allan Poe, author," and regularly posts notices of events, publications, quotations and art related to Poe's work, and has over three million "likes." Another, listed as "Edgar Allan Poe: Evermore" posts more history-based items and photos. At the time of this publication, its profile picture featured Jeff Jerome, the former curator of the Poe House and Museum, and the page has nearly ninety-seven thousand "likes."

A Twitter account listed as "Edgar Allan Poe" has over one hundred thousand followers and includes almost daily tweets. Many contain a statement of dark humor, such as this one from February 16, 2015: "In many ways being a frozen corpse is preferable to being a damp squishy one." The Edgar Allan Poe account on Instagram includes Poe-themed art, photos of Poe action-figures, and quotations. It currently shows over eight thousand followers.

POE IN THE NFL

In 1996 Baltimore was looking for a name for its new professional football team. A newspaper conducted a poll asking fans for their feedback. An overwhelming majority chose to honor the poet buried in their city and his most famous poem; the new team would be the Ravens. There are three mascots cheering at Ravens games: Edgar, Allan, and Poe.

This statue of Poe was unveiled in Boston in 2014. The life-size Poe is accompanied by a raven, a nod to his most famous poem and the poet's nickname.

For many years, a mysterious visitor would arrive at Poe's grave in Baltimore before dawn on the author's birthday, January 19. He would place three roses and a bottle of cognac on the grave and raise a toast. His identity was never discovered, and his last visit was in 2009, the two hundredth anniversary of Poe's birth. Although the mysterious "Poe toaster" no longer makes his annual visit, thousands of others come to Poe's grave each year to pay tribute to the mysterious author of "The Raven."

Vincent Buranelli said that if a survey of all the artists and works influenced by Poe was ever completed, "Poe would be revealed for what he is—America's greatest writer, and the American writer of greatest significance in world literature."[19]

CHRONOLOGY

1809– Edgar Poe is born on January 19 in Boston.

1827– First book, *Tamerlane and Other Poems*, is published, although the cover shows the unnamed author as only "A Bostonian."

1829– *Al Aaraaf, Tamerlane, and Minor Poems* is published.

1831– *Poems* is published.

1836– Begins work as editor for *Southern Literary Messenger*. At age twenty-seven, marries Virginia Clemm (age thirteen) on May 16.

1838– *The Narrative of Arthur Gordon Pym* is published.

1839– *The Conchologist's First Book* is published in Philadelphia.

1839–1840– Works as editor at *Burton's Gentleman's Magazine*.

1840– *Tales of the Grotesque and Arabesque* is published.

1841–1842– Works as editor for *Graham's Magazine*.

1843– *Prose Romances of Edgar A. Poe* is published. Wins contest with his story "The Gold Bug."

1844– Begins work at *Evening Mirror* in New York.

1845– "The Raven" is first published and becomes an immediate success. Works as editor, then owner of *Broadway Journal*.

1845– *The Raven and Other Poems* is published.

1845– *Tales* is published.

1847– Virginia Poe dies of tuberculosis on January 30.

1849– Poe dies in Baltimore on October 7.

1850– *Works of the Late Edgar Allan Poe,* edited by Rufus Griswold, is published.

1860– *Edgar Poe and His Critics* by Sarah Helen Whitman, Poe's former fiancée, is published. Her book is a defense of Poe.

1875– The Poe Memorial in Baltimore is dedicated on November 17.

1910– Poe is inducted into the Hall of Fame in New York.

1946– The Mystery Writers of America give the first Edgar Awards.

2009– Poe's 200th birthday. The unidentified "Poe Toaster" makes his last trip to Poe's grave on January 19.

CHAPTER NOTES

Chapter 1. Poe: Genius or "Jingle Man"?

1. Edgar Allan Poe, "The Raven," reprinted from *The Evening Mirror* (New York), January 29, 1845, *Edgar Allan Poe Society of Baltimore*, October 7, 2011, http://www.eapoe.org/works/poems/ravenb.htm.

2. Lei Jin, "Poe's Landscape: Dreams, Nightmares, and Enclosed Gardens," *Forum for World Literature Studies* 5, issue 1 (April 2013): 38.

3. Walt Whitman, "Edgar Poe's Significance," *Critical Essays on Edgar Allan Poe,* ed. Eric W. Carlson (Boston: G. K. Hall, 1987), 83.

4. Edgar Allan Poe, "Philosophy of Composition," *The Complete Works of Edgar Allan Poe, Volume XIV, Essays and Miscellanies*, ed. James A. Harrison (New York: AMS Press, 1965), 198.

5. Poe, "Philosophy of Composition," 201.

6. Bettina L. Knapp, *Edgar Allan Poe* (New York: Frederick Ungar, 1984), 89.

7. Edgar A. Poe, "Review of Hawthorne—Twice Told Tales," *Edgar Allan Poe Society of Baltimore*, June 19, 2013, http://www.eapoe.org/works/criticsm/gm542hn1.htm.

8. Arthur Hobson Quinn, *Edgar Allan Poe: A Critical Biography* (Baltimore: Johns Hopkins University Press, 1998), 335.

9. Henry James, "Comments," *Critical Essays on Edgar Allan Poe*, ed. Eric W. Carlson (Boston: G. K. Hall, 1987), 82.

10. Edmund Wilson, "Poe as a Literary Critic," *Critical Essays on Edgar Allan Poe*, ed. Eric W. Carlson (Boston: G. K. Hall, 1987), 109.

11. Margaret Fuller, "Review of "The Raven" and Other Poems," *Critical Essays on Edgar Allan Poe*, ed. Eric W. Carlson (Boston: G. K. Hall, 1987), 39.

12. Elizabeth Barrett, Letter to Edgar Poe, April 1846, *The Life of Edgar Allan Poe: Personal and Literary*, ed. George E. Woodberry (New York: Biblo and Tannen, 1965), 164.

13. Vincent Buranelli, *Edgar Allan Poe* (Boston: Twayne Publishers, 1977), 130–131.

Chapter 2. The Young Poet

1. Kenneth Silverman, *Edgar A. Poe: Mournful and Never-ending Remembrance* (New York: HarperPerennial, 1992), 3–4.

2. Hervey Allen, *Israfel: The Life and Times of Edgar Allen Poe* (New York: Farrar & Rinehart, 1934), 10–11.

3. "Poe Chronology," *Edgar Allan Poe Society of Baltimore*, February 26, 2012, http://www.eapoe.org/geninfo/poechron .htm.

4. Silverman, 17.

5. Arthur Hobson Quinn, *Edgar Allan Poe: A Critical Biography* (Baltimore: Johns Hopkins University Press, 1998), 83–84.

6. George E. Woodberry, *The Life of Edgar Allan Poe: Personal and Literary* (New York: Biblo and Tannen, 1965), 1:28–29.

7. Quinn, 90.

8. Ibid, 89.

9. Ibid, 110–112.

10. Matt Kelly, "At the University of Virginia, The Spirit of Poe Resides Evermore," *UVA Today*, July 14, 2011, https://news. virginia.edu/content/university-virginia-spirit-poe-resides-evermore.

11. "Tamerlane and Other Poems," *Edgar Allan Poe Society of Baltimore*, October 25, 2014, http://www.eapoe.org/works/editions/taop.htm.

12. Philip Beidler, "Soldier Poe," *The Midwest Quarterly* 53, issue 4 (Summer 2012): 334.

13. Allen, 187, 190.

14. John Neal, Notice in *Boston Ladies' Magazine*, in I. M. Walker, *Edgar Allan Poe: The Critical Heritage*. (London: Routledge & Kegan Paul, 1986), 69.

15. Woodberry, 72–73.

16. T. W. Gibson, "Poe at West Point," *Harper's New Monthly Magazine* XXXV, no. CCX (November 1867): 756.

17. Gibson, 755.

Chapter 3. Launching a Literary Career

1. Daniel Hoffman, *Poe Poe Poe Poe Poe Poe Poe* (New York: Anchor Press/Doubleday, 1973), 31.

2. Arthur Hobson Quinn, *Edgar Allan Poe: A Critical Biography* (Baltimore: Johns Hopkins University Press, 1998), 122.

3. "Poems of 1831," *Poe Museum*, 2014, www.poemuseum.org/collection-details.php?id=15.

4. Bettina L. Knapp, *Edgar Allan Poe* (New York: Frederick Ungar, 1984), 56.

5. Edgar Allan Poe, "Tamerlane," section IV, *Edgar Allan Poe Society of Baltimore*, April 9, 2010, http://www.eapoe.org/works/poems/tamerlnf.htm (June 22, 2015).

6. Ibid., section XI.

7. Ibid., section IX.

8. Quinn, 156.

9. Edgar Allan Poe, "Al Aaraaf," *Edgar Allan Poe Society of Baltimore*, September 28, 2013, http://www.eapoe.org/works/poems/aaraafe.htm.

10. Ibid.

11. Scott Peeples, *Edgar Allan Poe Revisited* (New York: Twayne Publishers, 1998), 12.

12. Ibid., 13.

13. Hoffman, 40.

14. Ibid., 60.

15. Knapp, 70.

16. Aldous Huxley, Letter to Paul Valéry, March 11, 1929, *Letters of Aldous Huxley*, ed. Grover Smith (New York: Harper and Row, 1969), 308.

17. Quinn, 86.

18. Edward H. Davidson, *Poe: A Critical Study* (Cambridge, Mass.: Belknap Press, 1957), 32.

19. Philip Van Doren Stern, ed., *The Indispensable Edgar Allan Poe* (New York: Book Society, 1950), 605.

20. Quinn, 179.

21. Ibid., 178.

22. Peeples, 22.

23. Vincent Buranelli, *Edgar Allan Poe* (Boston: Twayne Publishers, 1977), 100.

24. John Neal, Notice in *The Morning Courier and New York Enquirer, Edgar Allan Poe: The Critical Heritage*, ed. I. M. Walker (London: Routledge & Kegan Paul, 1986), 76.

Chapter 4. Author, Critic, Editor

1. Arthur Hobson Quinn, *Edgar Allan Poe: A Critical Biography* (Baltimore: Johns Hopkins University Press, 1998), 197.

2. Bettina L. Knapp, *Edgar Allan Poe* (New York: Frederick Ungar Publishing, 1984), 24.

3. Quinn, 212.

4. George E. Woodberry, *The Life of Edgar Allan Poe: Personal and Literary* (New York: Biblo and Tannen, 1965), 166–167.

5. Ibid., 171.

6. Ibid., 172.

7. Quinn, 239.

8. Ibid., 224.

9. Jeffrey Meyers, *Edgar Allan Poe: His Life and Legacy* (New York: Charles Scribner's Sons, 1992), 86.

10. Ibid., 259.

11. Edgar Poe, Letter to Joseph Evans Snodgrass, April 1, 1841, *Letters of Edgar Allan Poe*, ed. John Ostrom (New York: Gordian Press, 1966), 1:156.

12 John H. Ingram, *Edgar Allan Poe: His Life, Letters, and Opinions* (New York, AMS Press, 1965), 117.

13. Quinn, 251.

14. Kenneth Silverman, *Edgar A. Poe: Mournful and Never-ending Remembrance* (New York: HarperPerennial, 1992), 137.

15. Woodberry, 199.

16. Silverman, 138.

17. Quinn, 251.

18. Silverman, 154.

19. Quinn, 288–289.

Chapter 5. Poe's Premiere: *Tales of the Grotesque and Arabesque*

1. Edgar Allan Poe, Preface to *Tales of the Grotesque and Arabesque. Edgar Allan Poe Society of Baltimore,* March 6, 2010, http://www.eapoe.org/works/misc/tgap.htm.

2. Unsigned notice in the *Boston Morning Post, Edgar Allan Poe: The Critical Heritage*, ed. I. M. Walker (London: Routledge & Kegan Paul, 1986), 124.

3. Louis Fitzgerald Tasistro, "A Notice of Poe's Tales," *Critical Essays on Edgar Allan Poe*, ed. Eric W. Carlson (Boston: G. K. Hall, 1987), 36.

4. Unsigned notice in the New York *Alexander's Weekly Messenger*, Walker, 125.

5. Vincent Buranelli, *Edgar Allan Poe* (Boston: Twayne Publishers, 1977), 78.

6. Edgar A. Poe, "Review of Hawthorne—Twice Told Tales," *Edgar Allan Poe Society of Baltimore*, June 19, 2013, http://www.eapoe.org/works/criticsm/gm542hn1.htm.

7. Edgar Allan Poe, "Fall of the House of Usher," *The Tell-Tale Heart and Other Writings by Edgar Allan Poe* (New York: Bantam Books, 1988). All subsequent excerpts from "Fall of the House of Usher" come from this edition.

8. Scott Peeples, *Edgar Allan Poe Revisited* (New York: Twayne Publishers, 1998), 86.

9. John S. Hill, "The Dual Hallucination in 'The Fall of the House of Usher,'" *Twentieth Century Interpretations of Poe's Tales*, ed. William L. Howarth (Upper Saddle River, N.J.: Prentice Hall, 1971), 56.

10. Richard Wilbur, "The House of Poe," *Poe: A Collection of Critical Essays*, ed. Robert Regan (Upper Saddle River, N.J.: Prentice Hall, 1967), 108.

11. Clark Griffith, "Poe and the Gothic," *Critical Essays on Edgar Allan Poe*, ed. Eric W. Carlson (Boston: G. K. Hall, 1987), 130.

12. I. M. Walker in Howarth, 50.

13. D. H. Lawrence, "Edgar Allan Poe," *Critical Essays on Edgar Allan Poe*, ed. Eric W. Carlson (Boston: G. K. Hall, 1987), 97–100.

14. Louise J. Kaplan, "The Perverse Strategy in 'The Fall of the House of Usher," *New Essays on Poe's Major Tales*, ed. Kenneth Silverman (New York: Cambridge University Press, 1993), 62–64.

15. G. R. Thompson, "Explained Gothic," *Critical Essays on Edgar Allan Poe*, ed. Eric W. Carlson (Boston: G. K. Hall, 1987), 144.

16. Edgar Poe to Lea & Blanchard, August 13, 1841, *Letters of Edgar Allan Poe*, ed. John Ostrom (New York: Gordian Press, 1966), 1:178.

17. "Tales of the Grotesque and Arabesque," *Edgar Allan Poe Society of Baltimore*, July 7, 2001, http://www.eapoe.org/works/editions/tga.htm.

Chapter 6. The Struggling Writer

1. Kenneth Silverman, *Edgar A. Poe: Mournful and Never-ending Remembrance* (New York: HarperPerennial, 1992), 152.

2. Arthur Hobson Quinn, *Edgar Allan Poe: A Critical Biography* (Baltimore: Johns Hopkins University Press, 1998), 304.

3. Ibid., 305.

4. Edgar Poe, Letter to Joseph Evans Snodgrass, April 1, 1841, *Letters of Edgar Allan Poe*, ed. John Ostrom (New York: Gordian Press, 1966), 1:157.

5. Hervey Allen, *Israfel: The Life and Times of Edgar Allan Poe* (New York: Farrar & Rinehart, 1934), 387.

6. Quinn, 356.

7. Allen, 388.

8. John H. Ingram, *Edgar Allan Poe: His Life, Letters, and Opinions* (New York, AMS Press, 1965), 174.

9. Edgar Poe, Letter to Frederick W. Thomas, May 25, 1842, *Letters of Edgar Allan Poe*, ed. John Ostrom (New York: Gordian Press, 1966), 1:197.

10. Dwight Thomas and David K. Jackson, *The Poe Log: A Documentary Life of Edgar Allan Poe, 1809–1849* (Boston: G. K. Hall & Co., 1987), 375.

11. Thomas and Jackson, 441.

12. Jeffrey Meyers, *Edgar Allan Poe: His Life and Legacy* (New York: Charles Scribner's Sons, 1992), 151.

13. Edward H. Davison, *Poe: A Critical Study* (Cambridge, Mass.: Belknap Press, 1957), 101.

14. Quinn, 439.

15. Bettina L. Knapp, *Edgar Allan Poe* (New York: Frederick Ungar Publishing, 1984), 34.

Chapter 7. The Master Storyteller

1. "Poe's Writings in the Casket," *Edgar Allan Poe Society of Baltimore*, December 24, 2014, http://www.eapoe.org/works/editions/mgm001c.htm.

2. Bettina L. Knapp, *Edgar Allan Poe* (New York: Frederick Ungar Publishing, 1984), 144.

3. Harry Levin, *The Power of Blackness: Hawthorne, Poe, Melville* (New York: Vintage Books, 1958), 150.

4. Joseph Patrick Roppolo, "Meaning and 'The Masque of the Red Death,'" *Poe: A Collection of Critical Essays*, ed. Robert Regan (Upper Saddle River, N.J.: Prentice Hall, 1967), 140.

5. Ibid., 142.

6. Ibid.

7. Scott Peeples, *Edgar Allan Poe Revisited* (New York: Twayne Publishers, 1998), 104.

8. Hervey Allen, *Israfel: The Life and Times of Edgar Allan Poe* (New York: Farrar & Rinehart, 1934), 454.

9. Levin, 146.

10. Dwight Thomas and David K. Jackson, *The Poe Log: A Documentary Life of Edgar Allan Poe, 1809–1849* (Boston: G. K. Hall & Co., 1987), 389.

11. Arthur Hobson Quinn, *Edgar Allan Poe: A Critical Biography* (Baltimore: Johns Hopkins University Press, 1998), 430.

12. Edgar Allan Poe, "Tell-Tale Heart," *The Tell-Tale Heart and Other Writings by Edgar Allan Poe* (New York: Bantam Books, 1988), 3.

13. Vincent Buranelli, *Edgar Allan Poe* (Boston: Twayne Publishers, 1977), 73.

14. Poe, 5.

15. E. Arthur Robinson, "Poe's 'The Tell-Tale Heart,'" *Twentieth Century Interpretations of Poe's Tales*, ed. William L. Howarth (Upper Saddle River, NJ: Prentice Hall, Inc., 1971), 101–102.

16. Peeples, 150.

17. Ibid., 148.

18. Buranelli, 77.

19. David S. Reynolds, "Poe's Art of Transformation: 'The Cask of Amontillado' in Its Cultural Context," *New Essays on Poe's Major Tales*, ed. Kenneth Silverman (New York: Cambridge University Press, 1993), 93.

20. Peeples, 148.

21. Reynolds, 99.

22. Ibid.

23. Peeples, 150.

24. Christopher Benfey, "Poe and the Unreadable: 'The Black Cat' and 'The Tell-Tale Heart,'" *New Essays on Poe's Major*

Tales, ed. Kenneth Silverman (New York: Cambridge University Press, 1993), 36.

25. Edgar Allan Poe, "The Raven," reprinted from *The Evening Mirror* (New York), January 29, 1845, *The Edgar Allan Poe Society of Baltimore*, October 7, 2011, http://www.eapoe. org/works/poems/ravenb.htm. All subsequent excerpts from "The Raven" come from this edition.

Chapter 8. His Own Worst Enemy

1. Arthur Hobson Quinn, *Edgar Allan Poe: A Critical Biography* (Baltimore: Johns Hopkins University Press, 1998), 455.

2. Edgar Poe, Letter to Frederick W. Thomas, May 4, 1845, *Letters of Edgar Allan Poe*, ed. John Ostrom (New York: Gordian Press, 1966), 1:286.

3. Dwight Thomas and David K. Jackson, *The Poe Log: A Documentary Life of Edgar Allan Poe, 1809–1849* (Boston: G. K. Hall & Co., 1987), 530.

4. Jeffrey Meyers, *Edgar Allan Poe: His Life and Legacy* (New York: Charles Scribner's Sons, 1992), 187.

5. Ibid., 188.

6. George E. Woodberry, *The Life of Edgar Allan Poe: Personal and Literary* (New York: Biblo and Tannen, 1965), 2:162.

7. Quinn, 501.

8. Edgar Allan Poe, "The Literati of New York City: Some Honest Opinions at Random Respecting Their Autorial Merits, with Occasional Words of Personality," *Godey's Lady's Book*, May 1846, *Edgar Allan Poe Society of Baltimore*, May 15, 2015, http://www.eapoe.org/works/misc/litratb1. htm.

9. Meyers, 174.

10. Quinn, 524–525.

11. Ibid., 528.

12. Hervey Allen, *Israfel: The Life and Times of Edgar Allan Poe* (New York: Farrar & Rinehart, 1934), 592.

13. Quinn, 539.

14. Meyers, 227.

15. Ibid., 225.

16. Allen, 612.

17. Edgar Poe to Sarah Helen Whitman, October 1, 1848, *Letters of Edgar Allan Poe*, ed. John Ostrom (New York: Gordian Press, 1966), 2:388.

18. Thomas and Jackson, 764.

19. Ibid., 780.

20. Quinn, 592.

21. Meyers, 236.

22. Edgar Poe to Annie L. Richmond, January 21, 1849, *Letters of Edgar Allan Poe*, ed. John Ostrom (New York: Gordian Press, 1966), 2:418–419.

23. Ibid., 419.

Chapter 9. The Last Poems

1. Dwight Thomas and David K. Jackson, *The Poe Log: A Documentary Life of Edgar Allan Poe, 1809–1849* (Boston: G. K. Hall & Co., 1987), 732.

2. Burton R. Pollin, "Dickens' Chimes and its Pathway into Poe's 'Bells,'" *Mississippi Quarterly* 51, no. 2 (Spring 1998): 218.

3. Edgar A. Poe, "The Bells," *The Indispensable Edgar Allan Poe*, ed. Philip Van Doren Stern (New York: Book Society, 1950). All subsequent excerpts from "The Bells" come from this edition.

4. Arthur Hobson Quinn, *Edgar Allan Poe: A Critical Biography* (Baltimore: Johns Hopkins University Press, 1998), 564.

5. Vincent Buranelli, *Edgar Allan Poe* (Boston: Twayne Publishers, 1977), 108.

6. Hervey Allen, *Israfel: The Life and Times of Edgar Allan Poe* (New York: Farrar & Rinehart, 1934), 638.

7. Buranelli, 106.

8. Scott Peeples, *Edgar Allan Poe Revisited* (New York: Twayne Publishers, 1998), 173.

9. Edgar Allan Poe to Annie L. Richmond, after May 5, 1849, *Edgar Allan Poe Society of Baltimore,* December 5, 2009, http://www.eapoe.org/works/letters/p4904280.htm.

10. Thomas and Jackson, 801.

11. Edgar A. Poe, "Annabel Lee," *Edgar Allan Poe Society of Baltimore*, December 21, 2009, http://www.eapoe.org/works/poems/annabela.htm.

12. Quinn, 606.

13. Bettina L. Knapp, *Edgar Allan Poe* (New York: Frederick Ungar Publishing, 1984), 96.

14. Edgar Poe, "Annabel Lee," 632.

Chapter 10. Poe's Final Days

1. Jeffrey Meyers, *Edgar Allan Poe: His Life and Legacy* (New York: Charles Scribner's Sons, 1992), 242.

2. Edgar Poe to Maria Clemm, July 19, 1849, *Letters of Edgar Allan Poe*, ed. John Ostrom (New York: Gordian Press, 1966), 2:455.

3. Dwight Thomas and David K. Jackson, *The Poe Log: A Documentary Life of Edgar Allan Poe, 1809–1849* (Boston: G. K. Hall & Co., 1987), 826.

4. Ibid., 826.

5. John Evangelist Walsh, *Midnight Dreary: The Mysterious Death of Edgar Allan Poe* (New Brunswick, N.J.: Rutgers University Press, 1998), 21–22.

6. Susan Archer Talley Weiss, "Last Days of Edgar A. Poe, *Scribner's* XV (March 1878): 713–714.

7. George E. Woodberry, *The Life of Edgar Allan Poe: Personal and Literary* (New York: Biblo and Tannen, 1965), 2:341–342.

8. Walsh, 89.

9. Ibid., 56.

10. John H. Ingram, *Edgar Allan Poe: His Life, Letters, and Opinions* (New York: AMS Press, 1965), 427.

11. Thomas and Jackson, 830.

12. Arthur Hobson Quinn, *Edgar Allan Poe: A Critical Biography* (Baltimore: Johns Hopkins University Press, 1998), 637–639.

13. Walsh, 100–102.

14. Meyers, 256.

15. "Edgar Allan Poe Mystery," University of Maryland Medical Center News Release, September 24, 1996," last updated June 13, 2013, http://umm.edu/news-and-events/news-releases/1996/edgar-allan-poe-mystery.

16. Natasha Geiling, "The (Still) Mysterious Death of Edgar Allan Poe," *Smithsonian.com,* October 7, 2014, http://www.smithsonianmag.com/history/still-mysterious-death-edgar-allan-poe-180952936/?no-ist.

17. Ibid.

18. Hervey Allen, *Israfel: The Life and Times of Edgar Allan Poe* (New York: Farrar & Rinehart, 1934), 675.

19. "Death of Edgar A. Poe," reprinted from *New York Daily Tribune*, October 9, 1949, *Edgar Allan Poe Society*

of Baltimore, October 13, 2011, http://www.eapoe.org/PAPERS/misc1827/nyt49100.htm.

20. Arthur Hobson Quinn, *Edgar Allan Poe: A Critical Biography* (Baltimore: Johns Hopkins University Press, 1998), 592.

21. Ibid., 37.

22. Ibid., 381.

23. I. M. Walker, ed., *Edgar Allan Poe: The Critical Heritage* (London: Routledge & Kegan Paul, 1986), 50–51.

Chapter 11. Evermore: Poe's Legacy

1. Jeffrey Meyers, *Edgar Allan Poe: His Life and Legacy* (New York: Charles Scribner's Sons, 1992), 168.

2. George Washington Peck in the *American Whig Review*, *Edgar Allan Poe: The Critical Heritage*, ed. I. M. Walker (London: Routledge & Kegan Paul, 1986), 353.

3. George Bernard Shaw, "Edgar Allan Poe," *Critical Essays on Edgar Allan Poe*, ed. Eric W. Carlson (Boston: G. K. Hall, 1987), 88.

4. Edward Zuk, "On 'The Poetic Principle,'" *Expansive Poetry & Music Online,* accessed June 23, 2015, http://www.expansivepoetryonline.com/journal/zukpoe.html.

5. Aldous Huxley, Letter to Paul Valéry, March 11, 1929, *Letters of Aldous Huxley*, ed. Grover Smith (New York: Harper and Row, 1969), 308.

6. "Poe's Literary Contributions," *The Museum of Edgar Allan Poe*, 2014, https://www.poemuseum.org/teachers-poes-literary.php.

7. Meyers, 282.

8. Meyers, 283.

9. Ibid., 283–286.

10. Beatriz Gonzalez-Moreno, "Approaching the Dupin-Holmes (or Poe-Doyle) Controversy," *A Descent Into Edgar Allan Poe and His Works: The Bicentennial,* eds. Margarita Rigal Aragón and Beatriz González Moreno (New York: Peter Lang, 2010), 59.

11. Ibid., 64.

12. Dennis R. Perry, "Imps of the perverse: Discovering the Poe/Hitchcock connection," *Literature Film Quarterly* 24, issue 4 (1996): 393–394.

13. Ibid., 394.

14. Pamela Staik, "Stephen King at Charlotte Cultural Center," *Talk Stephen King* (Blog), March 20, 2010, http://talkstephenking.blogspot.com/2010/03/edgar-allen-poe-and-stephen-king.html.

15. "Poe's Literary Contributions," *The Museum of Edgar Allan Poe,* 2014, https://www.poemuseum.org/teachers-poes-literary.php.

16. Ray Bradbury, *Zen in the Art of Writing,* (Santa Barbara, Calif.: Joshua Odell Editions, 1996), 15.

17. Angel Mateos-Aparicio Martín-Albo, "'The Horrors Are Not To Be Denied': The Influence of Edgar A. Poe on Ray Bradbury," *A Descent Into Edgar Allan Poe and His Works: The Bicentennial,* eds. Margarita Rigal Aragón and Beatriz González Moreno (New York: Peter Lang, 2010), 84-85.

18. "Poe's Enduring Fame," *Edgar Allan Poe Society of Baltimore,* February 4, 2009, http://www.eapoe.org/geninfo/poesfame.htm.

19. Vincent Buranelli, *Edgar Allan Poe* (Boston: Twayne Publishers, 1977), 136.

LITERARY TERMS

alliteration—Poetic technique using repetition of consonant sounds (example: "What a tale of terror their turbulency tells," from *The Bells*).

assonance—Poetic technique using repetition of vowel sounds (example: "molten-golden notes" from *The Bells*).

epic—Long poem that tells the story of a hero.

foot—A part of a line of poetry consisting of stressed and unstressed syllables. The foot is repeated to form a rhythmic pattern, such as iambic tetrameter or trochaic septameter.

iamb(ic)—Meter made of two-syllable units (feet), consisting of an unaccented syllable, followed by an accented syllable. (example: "The love li ness of lov ing well!" from *Tamerlane* [this sample line has eight syllables, or four iambs; accented syllables underlined]).

internal rhyme—Poetic technique of rhyming words within a line of poetry (example: "Deep into that darkness *peering*, long I stood there wondering, *fearing*," from *The Raven*).

lyric poetry—Short poem that expresses intense feeling. May be set to music.

meter—Pattern of rhythm in a poem caused by the repeating patterns of stressed and unstressed syllables.

onomatopoeia—Poetic technique of using words which, when spoken, make a sound like they describe (examples: "pop," "hiss").

rhyme scheme—Pattern of rhyming words at the ends of lines of a poem. These are shown by labeling words that rhyme with letters of the alphabet, beginning with A.

Repeated rhymes are marked with the same letter; new sounds are marked with the next letter of the alphabet.

Romanticism—Style of literature from the early nineteenth century that features the quest for beauty, imaginative plots which may include the supernatural, and emotion over reason.

septameter—A line of poetry containing seven metric feet.

stanza—Section of a poem that is separated from other parts.

symbolism—Use of an object or idea or stand for something else.

tetrameter—A line of poetry containing four metric feet.

Transcendentalism—Philosophy and style of literature that became popular in the mid-nineteenth century. Transcendentalists believed that the individual should search for truth through meditation that goes beyond reason to put him in touch with nature and with a universal spirituality.

trochee—A foot of poetry consisting of one stressed (accented) syllable, followed by an unstressed syllable.

Major Works by Edgar Allan Poe

Poems

"Al Aaraaf"
"Alone"
"An Enigma"
"Annabel Lee"
"The Bells"
"Bridal Ballad"
"The City in the Sea"
"The Coliseum"
"The Conqueror Worm"
"A Dream"
"A Dream Within A Dream"
"Dreamland"
"Dreams"
"Eldorado"
"Elizabeth"
"Eulalie"
"Evening Star"
"Fairy-Land"
"For Annie"
"The Happiest Day, The Happiest Hour"
"The Haunted Palace"
"Hymn"
"Israfel"
"Lenore"
"The Raven"
"Romance"
"Serenade"
"The Sleeper"

"Song"
"Sonnet—To Science"
"Sonnet—To Zante"
"Spirits Of The Dead"
"Stanzas"
"Tamerlane"
"To Helen"
"To My Mother"
"To One In Paradise"
"To The River"
"Ulalume"
"A Valentine"
"The Valley of Unrest"

Fiction

"The Angel of the Odd—An Extravaganza"
"The Assignation"
"The Balloon-Hoax"
"Berenice"
"The Black Cat"
"Bon-Bon"
"The Business Man"
"The Cask of Amontillado"
"The Colloquy of Monos and Una"
"The Conversation of Eiros and Charmion"
"A Descent Into The Maelstrom"
"The Devil in the Belfry"
"Diddling—Considered as One of The Exact Sciences"
"The Domain of Arnheim"
"The Duc de l'Omlette"
"Eleonora"
"The Facts in the Case of M. Valdemar"
"The Fall of the House Of Usher"
"Four Beasts in One"

"The Gold-Bug"
"Hans Phaall"
"Hop-Frog or The Eight Chained Ourang-Outangs"
"How To Write a Blackwood Article"
"The Imp of the Perverse"
"The Island of the Fay"
"King Pest"
"Landor's Cottage"
"The Landscape Garden"
"Ligeia"
"Lionizing"
"Literary Life of Thingum Bob, Esq."
"Loss of Breath"
"The Man of the Crowd"
"The Man That Was Used Up"
"The Masque of the Red Death"
"Mellonta Tauta"
"Mesmeric Revelation"
"Metzengerstein"
"Morella"
"Morning on the Wissahiccon"
"Ms Found in a Bottle"
"The Murders in the Rue Morgue"
"The Mystery of Marie Roget"
"Mystification"
"Never Bet the Devil Your Head"
"The Oblong Box"
"The Oval Portrait"
"The Pit and the Pendulum"
"The Power of Words"
"A Predicament"
"The Premature Burial"
"The Purloined Letter"
"Scenes from Politian"

"Shadow—A Parable"
"Silence—A Fable"
"Some Words With A Mummy"
"The Spectacles"
"The Sphinx"
"The System of Dr. Tarr and Prof. Fether"
"Tale of Jerusalem"
"A Tale of the Ragged Mountains"
"The Tell-Tale Heart"
"Thou Art the Man"
"The Thousand-And-Second Tale Of Scheherazade"
"Three Sundays in a Week"
"Von Kempelen and His Discovery"
"Why the Little Frenchman Wears His Hand in a Sling"
"William Wilson"
"X-Ing a Paragrab"

The Narrative of Arthur Gordon Pym of Nantucket

FURTHER READING

Bloom, Harold, ed. *Edgar Allan Poe*. New York: Chelsea House, 2006.

Lange, Karen. *Nevermore: A Photobiography of Edgar Allan Poe*. Washington, DC: National Geographic Children's Books, 2009.

Ocker, J.W. *Poe-Land: The Hallowed Haunts of Edgar Allan Poe*. Woodstock, VT: Countryman Press, 2014.

Poe, Edgar Allan. *Edgar Allan Poe: Stories and Poems (Classics Reimagined)*. Beverly, MA: Rockport, 2015.

Semtner, Christopher P. *Edgar Allan Poe's Richmond: The Raven in the River City*. Charleston, SC: The History Press, 2012.

Websites

Edgar Allan Poe Society of Baltimore

www.eapoe.org/

A comprehensive website with links to full-text versions of all of Poe's stories, poems, and magazine writings. Also includes critical essays, a full biography, and more.

The Museum of Edgar Allan Poe, Richmond, VA

www.poemuseum.org/about.php

Includes biographical information about Poe, pages for teachers and students, audio files, and even information about the museum's annual Young Writers' Conference.

PoeStories.com

www.poestories.com

Provides factual information about Poe, summaries of his stories, vocabulary, a gallery of fan art, Poe quotations, links to other sites, and more.

INDEX